GRATITUDE

First published in 2024 by
Red Stripe Press
Upper Floor, Unit B3
Hume Centre, Hume Avenue Park
West Industrial Estate, Dublin 12, Ireland
www.redstripepress.com

© 2024 Sr Stanislaus Kennedy

All rights reserved. Without limiting the rights under copyright reserved alone, no part of this publication may be reproduced, stored in or introduced into a retrieval system, or transmitted, in any form or by any means (electronic, mechanical, photocopying, recording or otherwise) without the prior written permission of both the copyright owner and the above publisher of the book.

Every reasonable effort has been made to secure permission for the use of all poems in this book. If you can identify any omissions or errors please notify the publishers, who will rectify the situation at the earliest opportunity.

ISBN: 978-1-78605-246-9

Set in Linux Libertine and Essonnes Display
Book and cover design by Alba Esteban | Alestura Design
Printed and bound in Spain

compiled by
SISTER STAN

GRATITUDE

TABLE OF CONTENTS

Introduction | Sister Stan 11
Returning Kindness | Adam Harris .15
Empathy Is a Gift | Aidan Gillen 18
Family | Andy Farrell 21
A Community of Gratitude | Angie Gough 24
Gratitude Вдячність ('Vdiachnist') | Anya Bazilo 27
Fostering a Culture of Gratitude | Avril Ryan 30
Everything They Do Is Magic | Barry Egan 33
Sunflowers | Brenda Power 37
The Power of Gratitude | Brendan Courtney 40
God Moments | Brian Killoran 43
'It Is Only with Gratitude that Life Becomes Rich' | Catherine Day . .46
The Simplest Things | Catherine Kelly 49
Maintaining Perspective | Colm Mac Con Iomaire 52
The Essential Truth | Colm Ó Mongáin 55
Voicing Gratitude | Conor Dillon .58
The Power of Unwavering Belief | Conor Pope 61
My Failures Make Me Who I Am | Corey McCarthy 65
The Greatest Gift of Wisdom | Damien Dempsey 68
Those with the Least Have the Most Gratitude | Denis O'Brien . .72
Appreciate What You Have | Denise Charlton 76
The Power of Peace | Derek Scally .79
Connections and Communication | Diarmaid Ferriter 82

Another Day in Paradise | Eddie Gilmore 85
Hope | Edith Cunningham 88
Cherish the Blessings in Our Lives | Ellen O'Malley-Dunlop . .91
Converting a Gratitude Sceptic | Emily Logan 94
The Rocky Road to Gratitude | Emily Quinn 97
The Transfer of Trust | Enda Kenny 100
The Family Glue | Fiona Looney. 104
Opening Up | Frances Fitzgerald 106
Daily Dose of Well-Being | Frances Ruane 109
The Call of the Sea | Fran McNulty 112
Maybe, just maybe! | Gary Mason 116
Giving Back | Gemma Hoole 119
Levelling | George Lee 122
Doing the Right Thing | Ger Deering 125
Gratitude Is Love | Gráinne Seoige 128
Centrality of Gratitude | Hichael Rashid 130
Be Loved | Harry Goddard 133
Making a Difference | Heather Humphreys 136
Finding the Space to Be Grateful in an Imperfect World | Ian Hyland 139
Gratitude in My Daily Life | Jane Ohlmeyer 142
Catching Apples | JD Buckley 145
Who Do I Thank? | John Clarke 147
My Grateful Place | John Cunningham 150
I'm Grateful For... | Justine McCarthy 153
Look for the Helpers | Kathy Sheridan 156
Shining a Light | Kevin Bakhurst 159
The Tide of Love | Leo Varadkar 163
Birdsong | Linda Cullen 164

What I Am Grateful For... | Lisa-Nicole Dunne 167
The Making of Me | Liz O'Donnell 170
The Strength of Connection | Louise Phelan 173
Gratitude Brings Happiness | Marie Farrell 176
The Gift of Joy | Mary Black 179
The Power of Education | Mary Canning 182
Taking a Minute | Mary Coughlan 185
Looking for the Positive | Mary Hunt 188
Saying Thank You | Matt Cooper 191
The Potential of Hope | Michelle O'Neill 194
Using the Tools You Have | Mick Clifford 198
Gratitude Empowers | Monica McWilliams 201
Grounding | Niall Muldoon 204
Finding Room for Gratitude in the Quest to Succeed | Niall Quinn . 207
Building a Warm Welcome | Niamh McDonald 210
Gratitude Corner | Noel Cunningham 213
Reap What You Sow | Norma Smurfit 216
What Makes Me Feel Gratitude? | Oisín Coghlan 219
Moments of Connection | Paschal Donohoe 222
Hedge School | Pat Boran 225
Being Raised in the Middle of the House | Pat Dennigan 229
memories | Pat Spillane 232
Living in the Moment | Paul Cunningham 236
Three Essential Elements to Life | Paul Johnston 239
Starting Small | Paula Fagan 242
Moving Colours | Rachel Collier 245
The Foundation of Optimism | Rachel Hussey 248
My Guiding Light | Rosanna Davison 251

The Joy of Friendship | Rosita Boland 254
Finding Home | Ross Lewis 257
Creating a Daily Routine of Gratitude | Seán Gallagher 260
Accepting a Constant Tension | Seán O'Sullivan 263
The Cycle of the Seasons | Síle Wall 266
The Power of Midlife | Sonya Lennon 269
It All Comes Back to Family | Stephen Kenny 272
Widening Our Circles of Compassion | Sylvia Thompson 275
A Unique Healing Power | Tom O Brien 278
Two Simple Disciplines | Tony Keily 281
Put Your Oxygen Mask on First | Victoria Smurfit 284
The Gardening Cycle | Will Wedge 287
A Good Day | Brother David Steindl-Rast 290
What do you feel gratitude for in your daily life? 296
Acknowledgements 300

INTRODUCTION

Sister Stan

A favourite saying of mine is by Brother David Steindl-Rast: 'We are never more than one grateful thought away from peace of heart.'

When I turn my attention to feeling grateful, I feel happy, I feel blessed, I feel at peace and my mind is at peace.

I believe if more people were grateful, the world would actually begin to change for the better.

You can't be grateful and hateful. You can't be grateful and selfish.

Gratefulness brings a lot of benefits for the individual and for the world.

Having compiled two books on *Finding Peace* and *Finding Hope*, I was deeply curious and interested, not quite how or where people found gratitude, but more I wondered about people's feeling of gratitude; the idea that gratitude is something that is expressed. It is something that isn't 'found' outside us, but comes from within and radiates out. It spirals and grows.

I asked over 90 people the question 'what do you feel gratitude for in your daily life?', and was overjoyed by how quickly and enthusiastically people came back to me, happy to be able to reflect on the idea and share what came to mind for them. People responded so easily and with such generosity. It was as if it was an opportunity for them to channel their feelings of gratitude and release them onto a page. It became a wave of gratitude. I thanked people for contributing, people thanked me for asking them – it was as if the feelings of gratitude were contagious!

The people I asked to write pieces for this book are from all walks of life. Some very publicly well known, others not so well known, but all of them people who have wonderfully expressed what gratitude means to them in their daily lives.

Some of the themes overlapped, and some were totally different, but all of them were clearly written, straight from the hearts of those who were happy to share what gratitude means to them, and how and where they feel it in their lives.

The contributors to this book all inspire us in their own different unique ways to cultivate gratitude, and to realise the joy and kindness and well-being that gratitude brings.

The individual inspiring pieces that were written have made this a truly inspirational book, and my wish for the readers is that their lives will be happier and better as they learn from the contributors to practice living gratefully.

I hope this book will become a companion to the readers as they move through life, and they reflect and think about what the contributors have written on gratitude and the various aspects of the gift that they speak about.

* * *

My intention is that this book will encourage other people to cultivate and nourish gratitude, and hopefully express that gratitude and allow it to grow and travel around their communities, and out into the world.

If we make a habit of starting or finishing our day with a passage from one of these essays, we will begin to see life itself as a gift, and we will be happier and make others happier, and make the world happier.

If each day we could engage in a basic daily practice, it would be enough to positively impact our own lives and the world around us.

This is a Grateful Practice

Pause when you first wake in the morning and rest for a few moments at the edge of your bed.
Take time to notice three things for which you can feel grateful, before anything has yet happened ...
Parts of your body
The air around you
Sounds
Dreams
Simply notice and appreciate three things.
Then go into your day happy.

'As we express our gratitude, we must never forget that the highest appreciation is not to utter words, but to live by them.'

JOHN F. KENNEDY

· GRATITUDE ·

RETURNING KINDNESS

Adam Harris

My mum always brought us up on the mantra of 'success is liking what you do', and I am so grateful to have the privilege of working for Autistic people, one of the most excluded and discriminated communities within our country. The reason I am grateful for this opportunity is two-fold.

Firstly, I am only able to do the work I do because my parents fought to give me the same chance in the late 1990s and early 2000s when awareness of Autism was still very low, and segregation, in the education system and every aspect of community life, was often based on presumption. Through my parents' advocacy for me, I was able to transition to mainstream education, grow up in my local community and ultimately go to secondary school independently. None of that happened by accident, but only because my parents, like so many parents within our community, refused to take no for an answer. Part of gratitude is being able to appreciate when others show you kindness and to return it, and that is why it's important to me that I work to ensure everyone who is Autistic gets the same chance.

Secondly, I am grateful to work for the Autistic community because it saddens me just how grateful our community members can be for things that others take for granted – being shown respect, being included, going to school, making friends or getting a job. Others would never be grateful for such mundane and reasonable expectations, and it has always bothered me that people would be interested in or celebrate the opportunities I have had, which would be unremarkable for any of my neurotypical friends. Enabling a family to get the support they need, showing others in the community the role they can play to empower and include, speaking truth to power or helping a person see their strengths, dignity and value are truly humbling experiences which remind me of a simple truth – everyone deserves the same chance, no more but no less.

Adam Harris is the founder and CEO of AsIAm, Ireland's national Autism charity. Adam founded the organisation based on his own experiences growing up on the Autism spectrum. Today, AsIAm provides support to those with Autism and their families, advocates on behalf of the community, and works to support public and private sector organisations and communities in becoming inclusive and accessible.

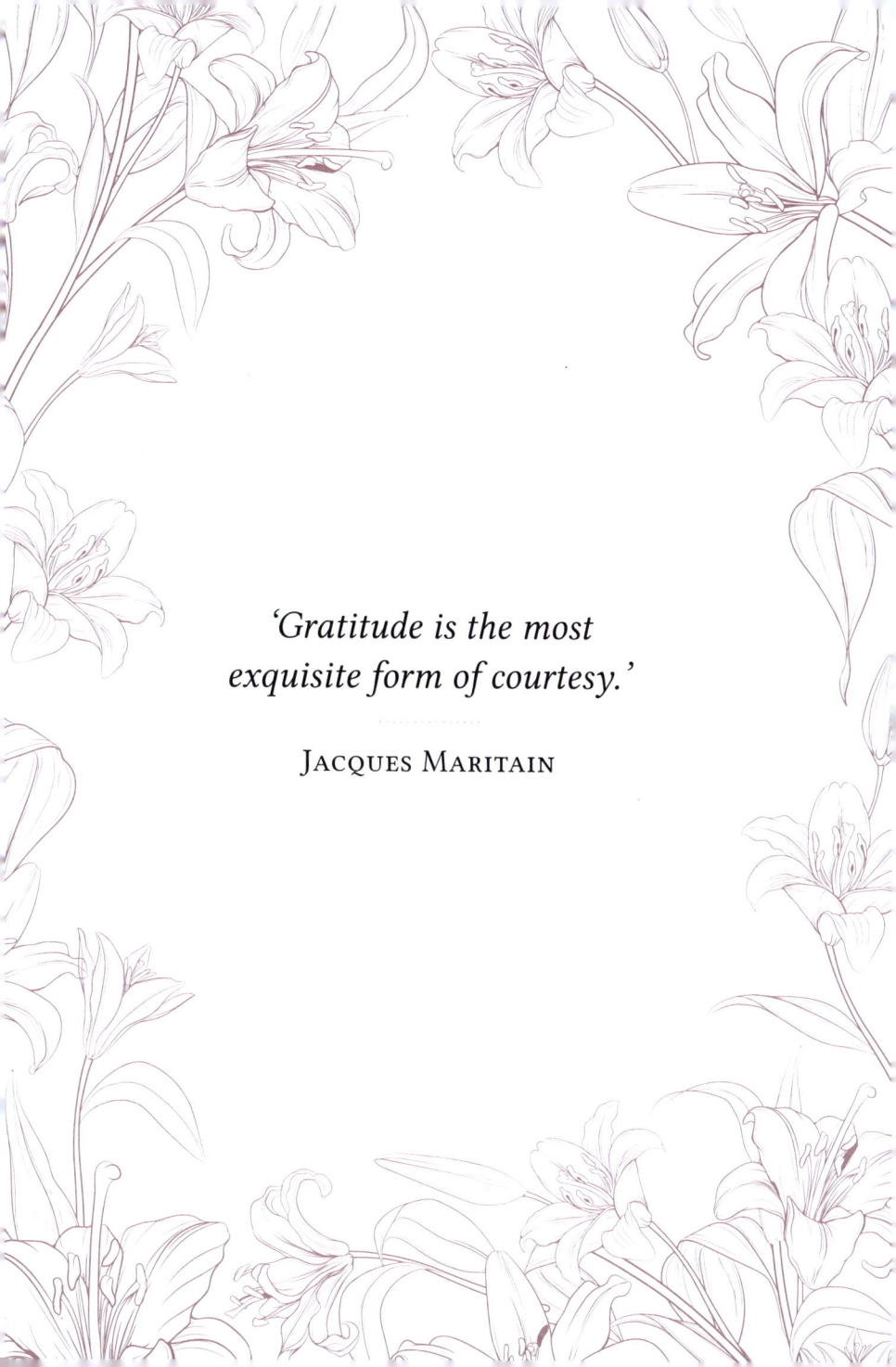

'*Gratitude is the most exquisite form of courtesy.*'

Jacques Maritain

EMPATHY IS A GIFT

Aidan Gillen

Three hundred words isn't much to be asked for on gratitude. I could list at least four hundred individual things I'm grateful for!

I suppose different things are obvious at different stages of your life, in different circumstances or places. Like when I lived in Kerry out west of Dingle some years back, what I was really grateful for and astounded by on a daily basis was the stunning natural beauty of the world as exemplified by that particular area, and having two young children to experience it all with. I'm grateful that I knew how lucky I was at that time, and therefore appreciated it even more. And children's eyes and questions help you see things you might not have been seeing or that you'd forgotten since you were a child yourself.

Or living in the city these days, and if you're lucky enough to have a comfortable place in which to live a healthy life you're grateful for that, seeing all the people who don't, sleeping on the street or queuing up for food outside the GPO or on Bow Street. And it's great that there are people out there looking and willing to help. Just people, wanting to look out for each other, whether it's as volunteers or nurses or just as good friends, these people are maybe what we should mostly be grateful for. Empathy is a gift – it's great to be taken care of, but it's also great to have others that you can take care of and try to ease their troubles in what can be a really difficult world to make it through for many.

I'm grateful to be able to lay in bed at the end of the day and read a few chapters of a book and sleep and dream – the human body, mind, imagination, subconscious are endlessly amazing, and I'm grateful to have been asked this question in the first place, because you can forget a lot of this, take it for granted, so it's nice to be nudged into reminding oneself to look after one's physical and mental health so we can make the most of our time living here on this earth, and the joy of sharing it with others.

And of course, I'm grateful to be living in a relatively stable part of the world while there are terrible wars raging abroad, making everything I've just described seem like extreme privilege, which it is, in comparison. So let's be grateful for peacemakers too, and hope they can find significant places at the table and help move us forward with reason and justice and light.

Aidan Gillen is an Irish actor. He is the recipient of three Irish Film & Television Awards and has been nominated for a British Academy Television Award, a British Independent Film Award, and a Tony Award.

'We can only be said to be alive in those moments when our hearts are conscious of our treasures.'

THORNTON WILDER

· GRATITUDE ·

FAMILY

Andy Farrell

A lifetime in sports teaches you many lessons. Highs and lows, peaks and troughs.

I feel privileged to work in sport as part of a team. As a player, there is nothing more satisfying than that feeling of working together and achieving collective success. As a coach, manager, teacher or leader, be it in any walk of life, the feelings are similar, but there is a special feeling watching people develop, overcome challenges and strive towards reaching their potential.

For the Ireland rugby team, family and community are at the heart of everything we do.

We all have our own back stories. Though born and raised in Wigan in northwest England, if you delve back a little bit in my own family tree, the Farrells' story began in Longford.

It's funny that three generations later, my family and I are back living in Ireland and grateful to meet new friends and experience memories that will no doubt last a lifetime.

The story of the Ireland rugby team mirrors that of the story of Ireland and its people. Our players and backroom team are a diverse group who come from towns and cities near and wide, and we are all united by our desire to represent Irish people to the best of our abilities.

There's a recurring familial theme here, but the things that I am most grateful for are my family and, above all, their health and happiness.

If you talk to people within the squad, family is at the heart of intrinsically who we are. We work hard and enjoy each other's company through shared accomplishment, and I am grateful to work with such a dedicated group.

· ·

Andy Farrell joined the Irish coaching set-up in 2016 as assistant coach. He was named as head coach after the 2019 Rugby World Cup. In 2022, Andy guided Ireland to their inaugural series victory in New Zealand. In 2023, he steered Ireland to our fourth Men's Grand Slam title and the Six Nations title a year later.

'Be grateful for what you already have while you pursue your goals. If you aren't grateful for what you already have, what makes you think you would be happy with more.'

Roy T. Bennett

· SR STAN ·

A COMMUNITY OF GRATITUDE

Angie Gough

When Russia invaded Ukraine in February 2022, I got caught up in the immediate response – first opening our family home to two women, their kids and a cat, then assisting others to do it too. Now I lead a team that is officially part of Ireland's national response, with a mission to channel, sustain and cultivate a community of people who opened their hearts and homes to people fleeing war.

It's a weird place to be, on the upside of other people's trauma and grief. When those two women arrived on our doorstep, shattered, in pieces, displaced, the pieces of my life fell into place. I experienced clarity, understood fully that I was exactly where I was meant to be, in the right place, at the right time, with the right skills, family and support network to meet the moment and harness it.

I'm profoundly grateful to have experienced a moment like that. Thanks to those two women.

My daily gratitude list is never-ending, written and unwritten.

From my journal: our house, a new jumper, gold foil curtains, a wind machine (birthday gift!), a painting, wildflowers in the garden, a holiday, places I've been. Grateful reflections on the place where

I am now. What a gift, what a lucky straw, to be born and to live in a free and peaceful country, where democratic values are upheld and a social safety net exists, and people and politicians genuinely care about minding the gaps, even if we don't always get it right.

So many names on the list. Husband, daughter, sons. Parents, siblings, aunts. People whose paths cross mine and make a mark – the dancer, actor, activists, artist, asylum seeker, musician, teacher, refugee, builder, flower seller, writer, politician, counsellor, surgeon, sister, refugee, brother, refugee, cousin, refugee, old friend, new friend, neighbour, refugee, poet, priest, piano player, potter, more refugees, people who entertain, uplift and inspire me. People close enough to give me hugs and kisses. Others who keep me lit with a nod or a wink or a wave. Or a heart emoji. ♥

Every day, I'm grateful to live in this part of the world, with its never-ending list of brilliant people, thankful for those I've met and the ones I haven't yet. Every day, I'm grateful for those two brave Ukrainian women who blew my life, my heart and my front door open.

Angie Gough is the CEO and co-founder of Helping Irish Hosts: www.helpingirishhosts.com.

'Rejoice always, pray without ceasing, give thanks in all circumstances; for this is the will of God in Christ Jesus for you.'

1 Thessalonians 5:16–18

GRATITUDE
ВДЯЧНІСТЬ ('VDIACHNIST')

Anya Bazilo

As a Ukrainian woman who found protection from war in Ireland, I have so many reasons to be grateful in this life. On 24 February 2022, my world was shattered by the outbreak of horrible and unjustified violence against my homeland. I could have lost everything that mattered to me: my family, my home, my country. Many people I knew did ...

Fortunately, I had some relatives who were already living in Ireland. They welcomed me to Dublin with open arms and helped me settle in. Having their presence and support in such a difficult time was priceless.

I also appreciate the warmth and generosity of the Irish people who received me and many other Ukrainians with respect and compassion. They made me feel at home immediately and gave me hope for the future. They showed me that there is still kindness and humanity in this world. This is a feeling I will never forget.

I am thankful for the peace, freedom and normality of life that I enjoy in Ireland. I can walk on the streets without worrying about missile attacks or hiding in bomb shelters. I can work, travel and socialise without restrictions or shortages of basic services. So many Ukrainians were offered shelter, assistance, education, employment and a chance to live a normal life. These are very basic things that we usually take for granted, but for so many people these things are now so special and valuable.

I am grateful for the new friends and community that I have found here. Establishing Ukrainian Action in Ireland and meeting a group of dedicated people who volunteer their time and energy to help others and help Ukraine win this war has been a blessing. Together we do amazing things and make this world a better place.

I am grateful for the opportunity to live my life and follow my dreams.

Most sincerely,
Anya

> Ganna (Anya) Bazilo is a co-founder of Ukrainian Action in Ireland – a charity with the mission to be the Ukrainian voice of action in Ireland. She has moved to Dublin because of the war in Ukraine. Ganna's professional background is in politics, communication and programme management.

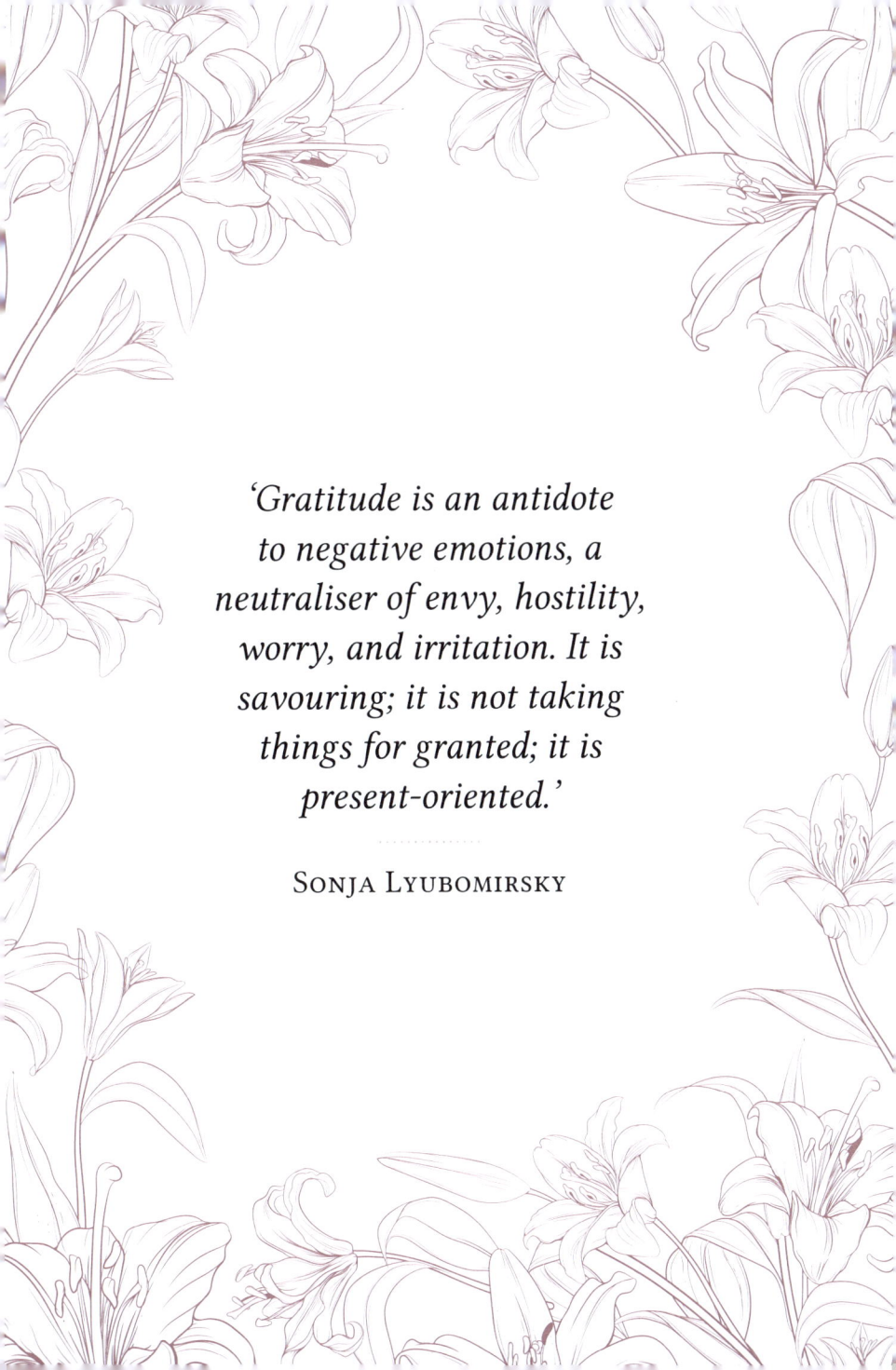

'Gratitude is an antidote to negative emotions, a neutraliser of envy, hostility, worry, and irritation. It is savouring; it is not taking things for granted; it is present-oriented.'

Sonja Lyubomirsky

· SR STAN ·

FOSTERING A CULTURE OF GRATITUDE

Avril Ryan

I am extraordinarily lucky to have a role where I get to share life-affirming stories about young people's achievements that capture the hearts and minds of everyone I meet. I am profoundly grateful for the journey my career has taken me on over the years, affording me the privilege of working in and leading organisations dedicated to empowering and uplifting young people. Being a champion for the rights of young people to flourish has enriched my own growth and joyousness. Leading an organisation that helps the youth of Ireland shape their own personal development pathways through non-formal learning gives me a great sense of purpose, drive and hope for the future, even when it seems to be a harsh old world. As CEO of Gaisce – The President's Award – leading with gratitude is core for me in what is very much a role that is about stewardship and cheerleading others to reach their full potential for the benefit of young people aged 13 to 25. Gaisce, Ireland's national youth development award, focuses on empowering young people to challenge themselves, develop skills, contribute to their communities, and embrace adventure by getting out of their comfort zone. My role involves not only strategic leadership to realise this ambition for young people, but also to foster a culture of gratitude, empathy and respect within the organisation. Having such a great team of like-minded colleagues, President's Award leaders and council members contributing to the success of Gaisce is invaluable, because every one of them believes in the vision Gaisce has for young people's participation in the programme, regardless of circumstance. That combined belief is the driving force that inspires collaboration, creates trust, and strengthens the outcomes we dream of for young people, so they have every chance to reach for the stars during these turbulent times.

Avril Ryan is the CEO of Gaisce
– The President's Award.

'In order to be happy we must first possess inner contentment; and inner contentment doesn't come from having all we want; but rather from wanting and appreciating being grateful for all we have.'

DALAI LAMA

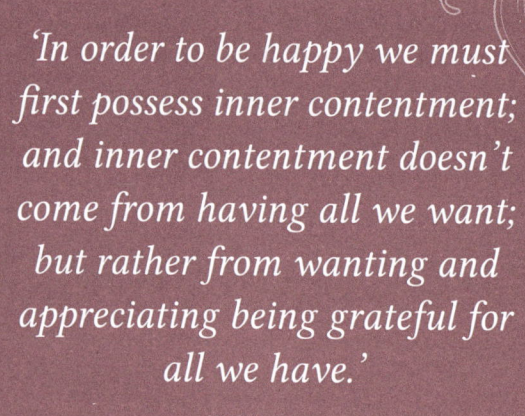

· GRATITUDE ·

EVERYTHING THEY DO IS MAGIC

Barry Egan

[Spoiler alert, if you are reading this with young children!]

They say there are three stages of a man's life:
1. He believes in Santa Claus.
2. He doesn't believe in Santa Claus.
3. He is Santa Claus.

I was grateful to become the plump, bearded saint who brings gifts on Christmas Eve night to my two young children. That sense of gratitude at having two great kids is present for longer than Christmas, of course.

To paraphrase The Police, everything they do is magic.

At the age of six, Daniel scores goals for fun when he plays football with his various teams. He scored 16 goals recently during a game. 'How many hat-tricks is that, Dad?' he asked when he came off the field in his tiny Manchester City strip. He wants to be the next Erling Haaland, and I don't doubt he will be one day.

I get more excitement watching him play with a bunch of six-year-olds in a field than I do watching the current Erling Haaland play against Manchester United on Sky Sports on a so-called Super Sunday.

Daniel's big sister, the incomparable Emilia, gives me just as much gratitude in life. At nine years of age, she is super-bright, super-smart, and super-brilliant at everything from gymnastics and dancing, to painting and reading. She likes to read out loud, like an actress at The Gate or The Abbey.

She loves Taylor Swift and, most of all, Billie Eilish. She sings and dances along to their songs in her bedroom. She knows all the words, and can add in her own words too. She will probably be the next Taylor Swift (or Saoirse Ronan).

I remember her coming down the slide in a play centre in Stillorgan when she was four. Suddenly, she said to me: 'Daddy, you don't need to hold my hand on the slide any more. I can get down myself.' I was wistful at the sense of something lost forever.

At nine and six years of age respectively, Emilia and Daniel are constantly moving to some new stage of their lives.

With them, life makes sense. It was as if (to paraphrase another song, this time 'Blackbird' by The Beatles) I had waited all my life for these moments to arrive.

Like me, they both love music, and I'd like to think are quite discerning in their musical tastes. In between asking big philosophical questions about existence, the planet and humankind – to say nothing of God – they love putting on their favourite tracks on the way to school each morning.

When they choose the tracks they want to hear, I feel overall a mixture of absolute joy and sometimes fear. The late Christopher Hitchens put it best: 'Nothing can make one so happily exhilarated or so frightened: it's a solid lesson in the limitations of self to realise that your heart is running around inside someone else's body.'

And yet, with a huge dollop of gratitude that I am blessed to have two amazing children to share life with.

．．．．．．．．．．．．．．．．．．．．．．．．．．．．．．．

Barry Egan has been on the staff of the Sunday Independent *newspaper since 1990. He has also written for* New Musical Express, Vox, Sounds *and* Company *in London,* Creem *in New York, and* Interview *in Paris. In 2016, he came up with the idea of the Rock Against Homelessness concert in aid of Focus. He was executive producer along with John McColgan of a concert in aid of Haiti (in the wake of Hurricane Matthew) at Dublin's Convention Centre in 2017.*

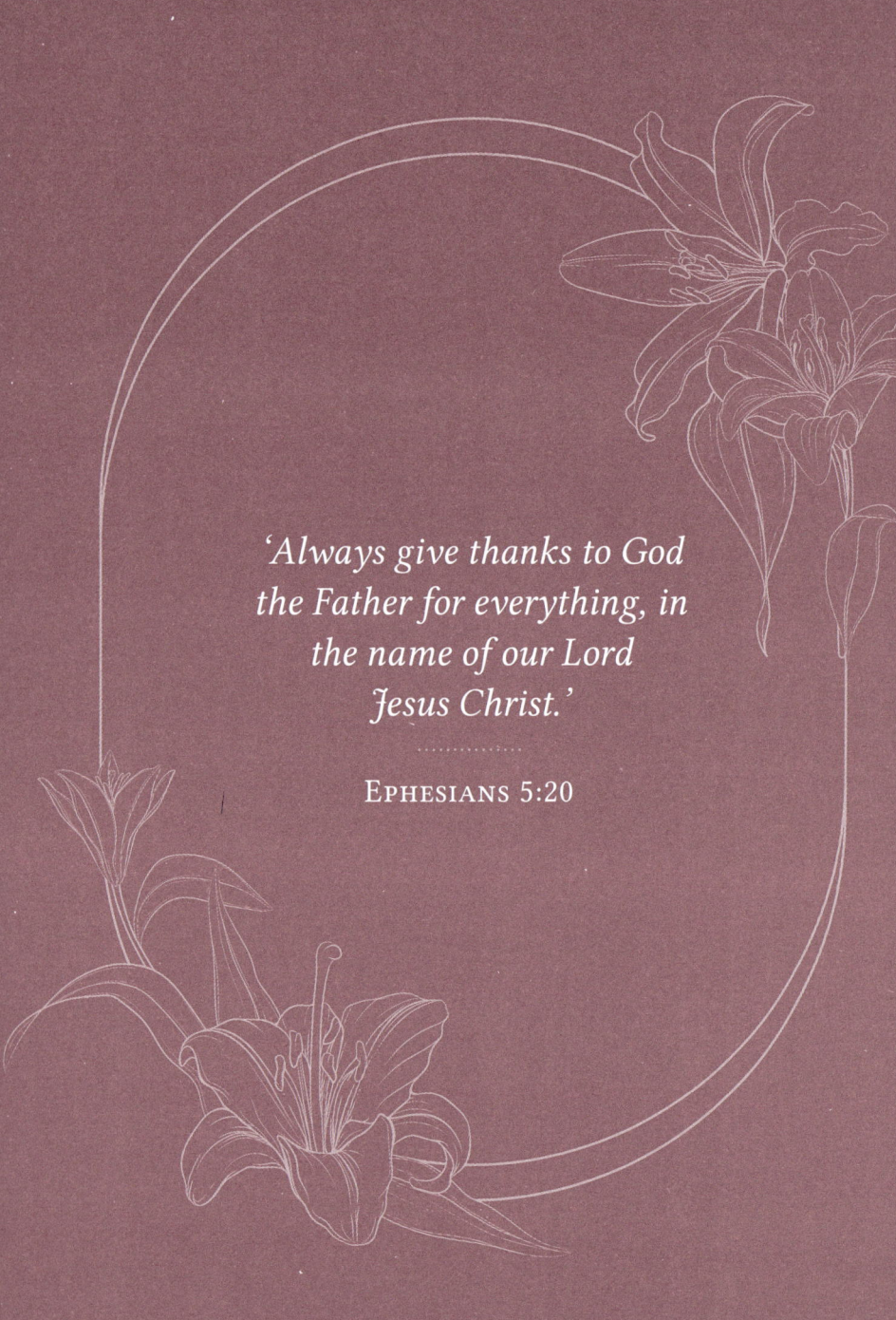

'Always give thanks to God the Father for everything, in the name of our Lord Jesus Christ.'

EPHESIANS 5:20

· GRATITUDE ·

SUNFLOWERS

Brenda Power

A few months ago, feeling a bit low as winter set in, I spotted a raincoat covered in bright yellow sunflowers in the *Irish Daily Mail's* fashion pages. It was half-price online, so I bought it straight away. I've practically lived in it since and, almost every time I've worn it, some passing stranger has admired it – one woman even stopped her car to ask where I got it. And every time I put it on, it 'sparks joy', although I do wonder if people are only admiring it because it looks a bit mad – the way you'd say 'I love your hat' to someone wearing a dead badger on their head.

Just today I wore it to hospital for a scan to investigate a nagging stomach pain, and wore it home again when the doctor told me all looked normal – and he even said he loved my coat! I am blessed with my family, I love them all beyond measure, and I would happily have taken a bad diagnosis if it was a choice between me and any one of them. But I know God doesn't do that sort of trade, and so I am grateful for my own good health, fingers crossed, and for my family's health, because nothing else in your life, no job, no money, no status, could possibly compensate if you lack it. And it's only when you get a fleeting scare, as you wait for the radiologist to say all's well, that you realise how much you take it for granted. I am immensely grateful that I have so few real worries in my life, for my family and loved ones, that all it takes is a dumb yellow raincoat, and a kind word from a passing stranger, to brighten my day.

· ·

Brenda Power is a columnist with the Sunday Times *and* Irish Daily Mail, *and also a regular contributor to radio and television current affairs panels. She is originally from Kilkenny but lives in Dublin, and has five children.*

'Train yourself never to put off the word or action for the expression of gratitude.'

ALBERT SCHWEITZER

THE POWER OF GRATITUDE

Brendan Courtney

When Sister Stan asks you if you would like to write a piece on 'gratitude' for her new book, what's the first emotion one feels? Without any irony, I felt immediately grateful and humbled that one such incredible human would even think of including me. It filled me with so much joy, love and, yes – gratitude. You see, Stan and I met when I was starting my TV career, before I was a presenter (all the while dreaming and scheming). I was a researcher on a daytime TV show called *Open House* in 1998, and Sister Stan was my guest. Upon meeting her, I instantly became fascinated with her and her work. One of the first things she ever said to me, during our pre-show briefing, was to ask me if I was grateful. It flummoxed me, and in my youthful naivety I quizzed back 'for what?' In her lovely quiet lilt, she replied: 'for everything'. Whether it was intentional or if it happened inadvertently, she started my life-long relationship with gratitude.

At the start, it began with taking stock when things seemed difficult, reminding myself of all the good in my life when I sometimes got frustrated; then it developed into a real sense of wonder of how the hell I got so lucky. Living in gratitude makes

· GRATITUDE ·

every day a bonus, every interaction a treat and every down moment an opportunity to learn. It is a frame of mind that just needs practice and, of course, we can slip back to old habits, but that's the wonderful gift of gratitude – it's always just sitting there waiting for you to re-engage. For me, it's like the unconditional love of my amazing dog – my relationship with gratitude feels just like that, and I am ironically so grateful for learning the power of gratitude, and to think my mind shifted all those years ago with a few choice words from Sister Stan – and here I am getting to thank her in print! How thankful am I!

. . . .
Brendan Courtney is a TV and radio presenter, and also one half of design duo Lennon Courtney.

'There is a calmness to a life
lived in gratitude, a quiet joy.'

RALPH H. BLUM

· GRATITUDE ·

GOD MOMENTS

Brian Killoran

I've always been interested in meditation and mindfulness, much the same way someone may have an interest in entering the monastery on top of the hill but can't work up the courage, so they eye it suspiciously every day as they pass. In my case, I'm 'too busy' to enter, or so I tell myself. Maybe I'll get into it next week, or the week after, or a month from Tuesday.

Our minds spend so much time caught in the past and the future – reaching out from the present trying to discern the way forwards, looking into a defective crystal ball. We expend untold energy trying to escape the present moment, and yet the present moment persists. It's always there. It's all there is; and in it, there opens a deep portal into the infinite.

There are times I get small glimpses. Moments when the past and future fall away, and there is a breath to be taken and a widening of awareness experienced. These, for me, are brief but profound glimpses into what meditation and mindfulness point us to. They most frequently happen with our children. I'll look at them, doing their chaotic thing, safe and happy and healthy, and for a moment I'll pause and breathe. They last, like, five seconds. But in those moments, I feel an overwhelming presence, a deep sense of peace, and a deep sense of gratitude. I have taken to calling them 'God moments' – even though I do not subscribe to the traditional concept of God that many of us were taught. For me, 'God' is this deep awareness, this interconnectivity, and an eye through which we can view the momentary and transient instances of our lives and see them as they truly are – miraculous and profound. For that I am grateful, as these instances anchor me in what really matters.

· · · · · · · · · · · · · · · · · · · ·

*Brian Killoran is the CEO of the
Immigrant Council of Ireland.*

*'Gratitude is riches.
Complaint is poverty.'*

Doris Day

'IT IS ONLY WITH GRATITUDE THAT LIFE BECOMES RICH'

Catherine Day

We are often advised to 'count our blessings'. I agree we should, but we should also give thanks for them. Those of us who live in Ireland today have so much to be grateful for: we live in a generally safe, prosperous country with a temperate climate; and a thriving democracy where, despite some shortcomings, the state is accountable to us.

I feel lucky to have been born into a loving family which valued education equally for girls and boys, and which has always supported me in everything I wanted to do. I have had good bosses and lots of opportunities to spread my wings and tackle new challenges.

Most of my 'luck' has not been down to me, but to people who took an interest, encouraged me or sometimes told me some home truths. As I get older, I realise the importance of being grateful for what I have and not taking it for granted. Counting blessings leads to a more optimistic view of the world than reciting woes.

We cannot always repay those who gave us the breaks or showed us kindness, but we can pass it on to others. I think that gratitude should lead us to take responsibility for sharing some of what we have. That may mean advocating for justice and social change, or supporting those in need. It may mean putting ourselves out to listen to someone when we are busy. Whether in the European Commission, chairing a Citizens' Assembly or working to end direct provision, I have always gained more than I gave. As Dietrich Bonhoeffer, the anti-Nazi German theologian, said: 'In ordinary life we hardly realise that we receive a great deal more than we give, and that it is only with gratitude that life becomes rich.'

Catherine Day was the first woman Secretary General of the European Commission. She chairs the Board of Trustees of the Chester Beatty Library. She chaired the Citizens' Assembly on Gender Equality and advises the government on ending direct provision for asylum seekers.

'For it is all for your sake, so that as grace extends to more and more people it may increase thanksgiving, to the glory of God. So we do not lose heart. Though our outer self is wasting away, our inner self is being renewed day by day.'

2 Corinthians 4:15–16

· GRATITUDE ·

THE SIMPLEST THINGS

Catherine Kelly

Life can change in an instant. As an oncologist, I am perhaps too familiar with this concept. Exposure to cancer has amplified my sense of gratitude for the simplest things – a cup of tea, a cosy bed, seasons changing, my daughter playing. I am grateful for the clarity of knowing what is and is not important. I am grateful through my work to have been able to help and alleviate distress through explanations and hopefully solutions, or through listening and accepting sometimes that that is all I can do. I am humbled and awed by the honesty, resilience and strength of the people I have had the privilege to get to know and treat. Understanding that life is short, and that we control very little, makes me face my own mortality and cherish every minute.

I am so grateful for my lovely family, for my friends, colleagues, and mentors, for the variety and hope in every day, and for education and the many opportunities it has given me. It has opened doors, and continues to expand and bring meaning to my world. I am grateful for scientific research and knowing that whatever part I play, however small, it's a piece of the puzzle that brings us closer to answers. I am grateful for love, laughter, fun and the excitement of not knowing what is around the next corner.

....
Professor Catherine M. Kelly is a consultant medical oncologist and UCD clinical professor at the Mater Private Hospital in Dublin.

'When it comes to life, the critical thing is whether you take things for granted or take them with gratitude.'

G.K. Chesterton

· SR STAN ·

MAINTAINING PERSPECTIVE

Colm Mac Con Iomaire

Gratitude is a world view.

A matter of raising our heads and looking around.

To be grateful requires perspective, and maintaining perspective is certainly a challenge in these accelerated times. To be grateful is to acknowledge our interdependence and the truth that we didn't get here by ourselves.

I learned recently that the number of direct ancestors (grandparents and great-grandparents) we all have stretching back just 400 years (12 generations) is 4,094.

Each and every personal link in that human chain is integral to our living present.

I am reminded of poet Paula Meehan's stunning line: 'Honey of survival in our ancestors' sweat.'[1]

In that context, another poet's epitaph – Seán Ó Ríordáin's – rings true to me.

---

1 From 'This Bed, This Raft on Stormy Seas', in *Museum* by Dragana Jurišić (photographer) and Paula Meehan (author) (Dublin: Dublin City Council Culture Company and Dublin City Council, 2019). Reproduced with the kind permission of Paula Meehan and the Dublin City Council Culture Company.

· GRATITUDE ·

It is a line from one of his poems, 'Toil' (Choice):[2]

'Níl ionam ach ball
De chorp san mo shinsir.'
'I am but a limb of that body, my ancestors.'

I believe that it is in living with and in that knowledge that burdens are lifted and blessings are bestowed.

> *Dublin-born, Wexford-based Colm Mac Con Iomaire is a violinist and multi-instrumentalist composer. He is a founding member of two well-known Irish bands, The Frames and Kíla.*

2 From 'Toil', in *Línte Liombó* by Seán Ó Ríordáin (Baile Átha Cliath: Sáirséal agus Dill, 1971). Reproduced with the kind permission of Cló Iar-Chonnacht.

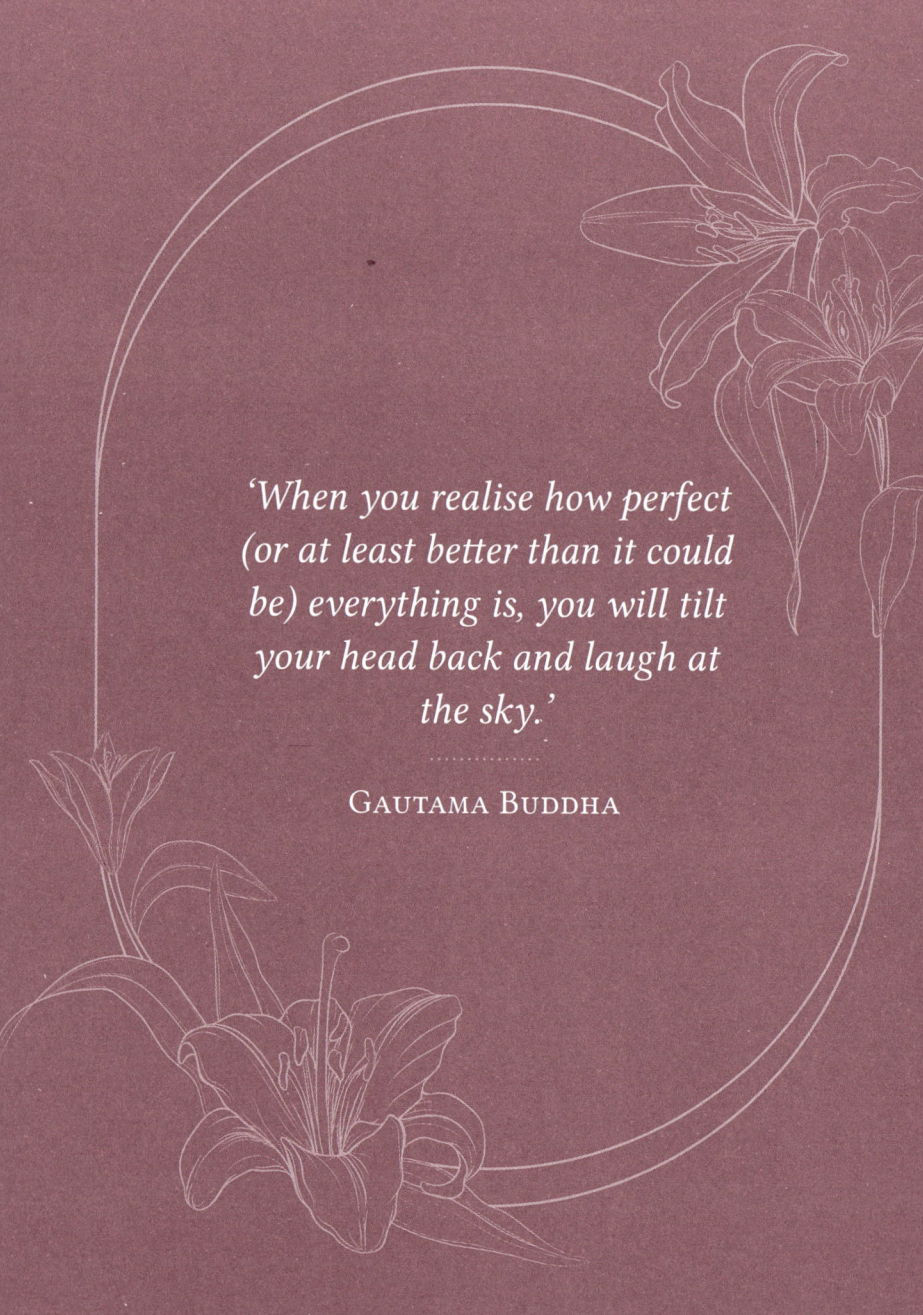

'When you realise how perfect (or at least better than it could be) everything is, you will tilt your head back and laugh at the sky.'

GAUTAMA BUDDHA

· GRATITUDE ·

THE ESSENTIAL TRUTH

Colm Ó Mongáin

Over the years I have worked as a journalist, I have been invited into homes and been allowed to record intimate – and sometimes painful – stories.

Survivors of traumatic events risk reliving the moments they never wanted to experience. People who have fought for years to highlight an injustice that they or maybe a loved one have suffered dig deep, past the memories of previous frustrations and disappointments, to find the hope that one more interview might help.

Those people who take the time to speak to me realise that an hour spent talking might only result in minutes of broadcast material. They have faith that, in editing their story, I will preserve the essential truth they want to tell. There is huge generosity in the trust interviewees show, one I have no right to expect.

I am only in the role of interviewer in the first place thanks to other people throughout my life, people who gave me the opportunities I have had, people who gave me first chances, more who gave me second chances, people who saw potential and showed patience, people who were willing to look past obvious flaws and see the better parts, people whose example made me think deeper and try harder, and people who were prepared to challenge me for my own good.

When the studio light goes red and people take the time – the risk – to share a story in an interview, it is only right that I feel gratitude for the trust placed in me by them and by those who support me to do the job I do.

· ·

Colm Ó Mongáin is an RTÉ journalist. He presents The Late Debate *and* Saturday with Colm Ó Mongáin *on RTÉ Radio 1.*

'If the only prayer you said was "thank you", that would be enough.'

Meister Eckhart

· SR STAN ·

VOICING GRATITUDE

Conor Dillon

My name is Conor Dillon and I live in Dublin. I was 2lb in weight when I was born and have quadriplegic cerebral palsy. I don't think many people expected me to do much with my life, but I'm enjoying proving them wrong.

I'm sure a lot of people don't think I have much to be grateful for. I'm quadriplegic, I'm on the mild end of the autistic spectrum, I can't write, dress myself, shower myself, cut my own food, or even clean my own teeth. But, they are very wrong. I have gratitude for plenty of things in my life. The first is life itself. Only for the fact that I was lucky enough to be born on this side of the world, where the hospital I was born in had the equipment and specialists I required, did I have any chance of life at all. There can be no greater gratitude than the gratitude for that.

I didn't speak until I was four years old. My parents were told I would never talk. I'm really glad that I can speak; at school, a lot of my friends were non-verbal. I advocate for other disabled people and have been on advocacy committees in the Youth Council of Ireland. I'm in a political disability group, and I'm a great man for spreading the word via charity bucket collections!

Independence is a huge struggle for people like me. I am very grateful that I have an electric wheelchair. It allows me freedom; I call my chair my 'legs'. It's great not having to wait for someone to push me, although sometimes I do need to be in a manual chair. Accessibility for wheelchair users is not perfect by any means … yet. I hope I can use my voice to help make the world a more accessible place for the next generation.

The world can be a very sad place. Wars, homelessness, poverty, injustice, sickness. The TV and radio spread gloom every day. In Ireland, I feel so sorry for people who are homeless. Anyone can become homeless. I have a lot of gratitude for a warm house and food every day.

Conor Dillon is an advocate for disabled people who has worked with the Irish Wheelchair Association and the Caring and Sharing Association (CASA).

"The steadfast love of the LORD
never ceases;
his mercies never come to an end;
they are new every morning;
great is your faithfulness.
"The LORD is my portion,"
says my soul,
"therefore I will hope in him.""

LAMENTATIONS 3:22–24

· GRATITUDE ·

THE POWER OF UNWAVERING BELIEF

Conor Pope

Not long ago, I got an unfiltered look into my past after finding a scribbled letter written by me to me in a battered brown suitcase left unopened for 25 years.

I wrote the note in the 1990s while on a FÁS computer course I'd signed up for as an alternative to signing on – my poor English and Philosophy degree rendered me mostly unqualified for anything and I had to do something.

The note dripped gloomy anxiety, and made it clear I was lost with no prospects, and unaware that one day I'd be writing this. The reason I am is my father. While I had no self-belief, he had it for me in spades, and after staggering through the computer course, I glided through a TEFL course and found my way to Spain.

Before leaving Ireland, I'd half-heartedly applied for a US Green Card and got one as I settled in a mining town in mountainous Spain. I liked being El Professor and didn't want the visa then; but, for a deferral, I needed the offer of a place on a post-graduate course.

Given my flaky degree, I reckoned an offer was beyond me, but my father disagreed. The course in journalism in Galway was still accepting applications, so he posted me the forms. They'd rejected me two years earlier on the legitimate grounds that I was a bad student, loved Hunter S. Thompson too much and wore a piano keyboard tie to the interview.

I knew applying was pointless, but my father persisted, so I filled in the forms, which he hand-delivered to the college. When he rang to say I'd been accepted, my life changed direction and pretty much everything I have now – my family, my job, my life – is down to his unwavering belief. I never thanked him properly before he died suddenly many years ago, but I am eternally filled with gratitude that someone believed in me when I didn't believe in myself. Too many people aren't that lucky.

****

Conor Pope is the consumer affairs correspondent with the Irish Times *and a frequent contributor to radio and television programmes in Ireland and overseas. He has fronted multiple consumer-focused TV series on both RTÉ and Virgin Media Television, and many years ago missed out on the final of* Celebrity Masterchef *because he put too much lavender in a dessert. It still rankles.*

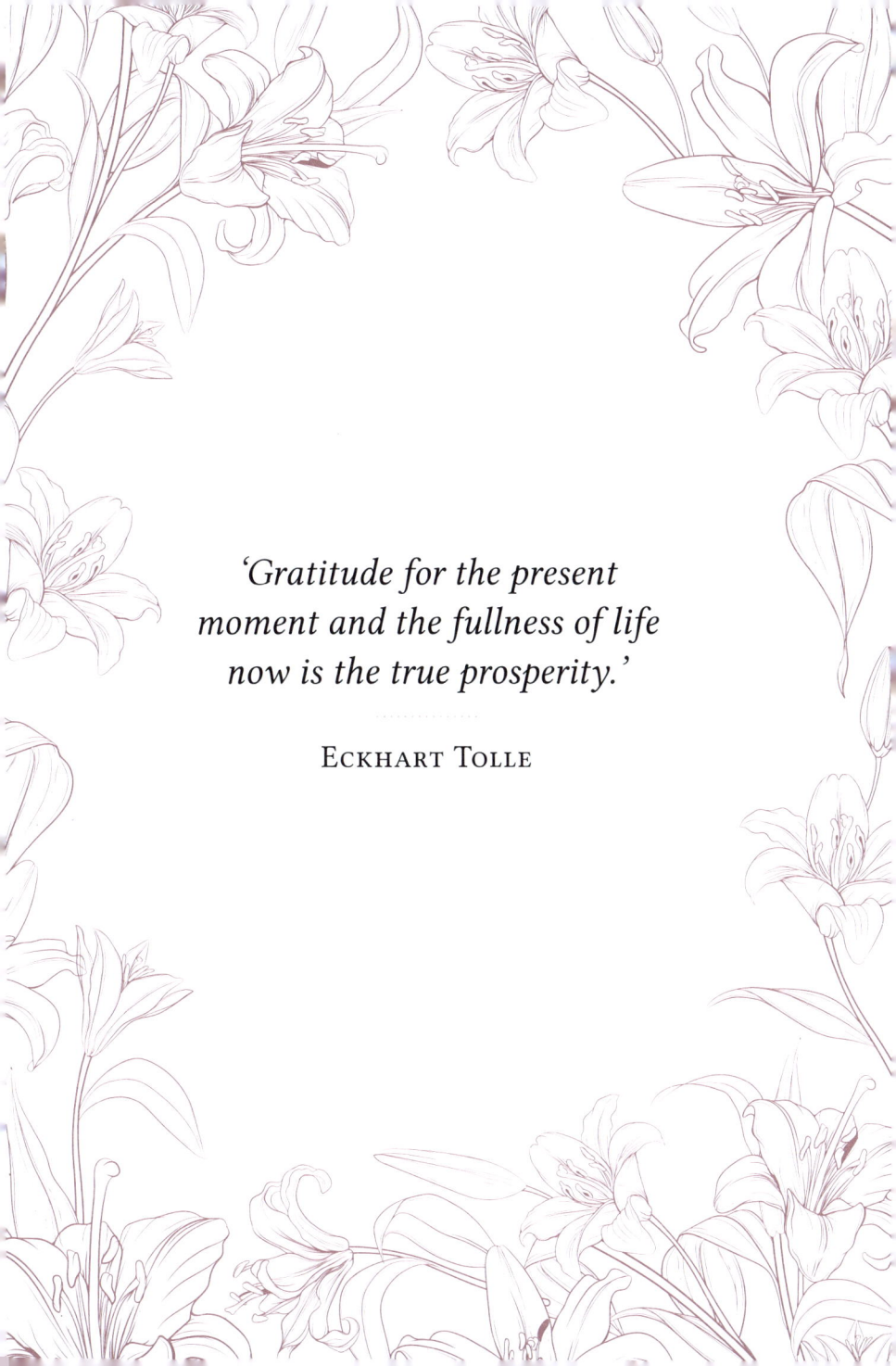

'Gratitude for the present moment and the fullness of life now is the true prosperity.'

Eckhart Tolle

'Count it all joy, my brothers, when you meet trials of various kinds, for you know that the testing of your faith produces steadfastness. And let steadfastness have its full effect, that you may be perfect and complete, lacking in nothing.'

JAMES 1:2–4

· GRATITUDE ·

MY FAILURES MAKE ME WHO I AM

Corey McCarthy

Hello, my name is Corey. I'm 18 years old and I am currently attending Terence MacSwiney Community College. I'm hoping to go to college and pursue a degree in political science in an attempt to change the trajectory of Ireland away from its destructive, hopeless and calamitous course.

I first became involved with Young Social Innovators (YSI) because of an interview with my school. YSI has been involved either solely or in part with competitions, events and conventions which we were encouraged to take part in.

It is when the small comforts in life are taken away that you realize how vital they were. Through experience, I have come to value the little things, like the ability to stay warm in the winter or to sleep knowing, with utmost certainty, that I will return the following night. This kind of security is something I cherish now. The ability to call a place mine. A place where no matter what happens during the day, I can always seek respite and solitude.

There is no greater feeling than community. It guards against all the negative emotions you can experience and when you are in need it is invaluable to have people to rely on. It might sound confusing, but I have become more self-reliant whenever I ask someone for help. I think this is because I have learned to apply the specific advice to a more general problem. Genuinely internalising people's advice to you will stop any patterns of over-reliance and will allow you to grow as a person. I say this because I have seen it from both perspectives as an outside observer: one, giving help without ever being asked; the other, because of this, being unable to grow as a person.

You might find it weird, but if I could go back and change everything I have ever regretted or done wrong I wouldn't. It is my failures and regrets that have made me who I am. While I am grateful for what I have in life, one thing I have learned is that nothing will be given to you. You need to work and claw for everything, and even then there will be people who will try and take this from you. That is why I truly emphasise community, unity and solidarity because if you can find people who are willing to help each other without a price tag, that is invaluable. I wouldn't have gotten anywhere without these people.

I would like to impart the most important ability I have gained and that is to question everyone. Why are some people prioritised over others, and why do some people never have to endure the same hardships as others? To say it in a different way, be grateful for what you have but always question those who say you can't have more. Question those who say you can't have it all because who are they to judge and to limit the lives of others? You can everything or as much as you are content with, but it will not be given to you so you must reach out and take it for yourself. Keep greed and avarice in check and help those around you because life is hard. But it is hard for us all.

....

Corey McCarthy is an 18-year-old student at Terence MacSwiney Community College. He hopes to pursue a degree in political science in third-level education. He first became involved with Young Social Innovators through an interview with his school. He has participated in many competitions, events and conventions involving YSI.

THE GREATEST GIFT OF WISDOM

Damien Dempsey

Thanks be to jaysus for gratitude is all I can say. Actually, I've more …

Gratitude has changed my life, the way I look at the world, and the way I think and feel about everything.

It's one of the greatest gifts of wisdom there ever was, a manna from the Great Spirit, Danu, God, whatever you want to call the light.

To properly start practising gratitude, I've found it takes time and perseverance, like anything worthwhile. You start to realise then after a while, with a big smile, that when you're truly grateful, it's a joyous feeling.

It's not forced or subservient, it's a warm glow within, so being grateful is a joyful way of life.

When you practice gratitude a lot, without fail, you'll find you get luckier. More good things come your way, and it's easier to help others, as you have more energy and resources and love to do so …

· GRATITUDE ·

When you give, you'll give with a full heart and feel good about it, and when you receive, you'll receive with a full heart and feel good as well, and you'll start giving more and receiving more.

It's like studying or boxing or a bank, the more you put into it, the more you'll get out of it.

Gratitude must become a mainstay in your life, like playing the guitar, or singing, or poetry, cooking, walking, etc ... You can't just try it for a fortnight and throw it there. You need to keep at it through failures and hard times until it's wedged in your heart and head, and then you'll be in love with it and never want to live without it, and it will be one of the greatest friends you've ever had and will never let you down.

There's a book called *The Magic* by Rhonda Byrne about gratitude, and she has tasks in the book to try to help the reader get into the mindset of practising gratitude. I just read through the book and circled passages that spoke to me, and now I open it at random every morning and read one or more of the passages, and it sets me on a better trajectory for the day.

She also speaks about how important gratitude was to all the tribes of the ancient world, and reminds us that every wise woman and man who are still studied and revered down through history all placed huge emphasis on the importance of gratitude.

I could never go back to feeling no gratitude for my eyesight, speech, hearing, smell, taste, legs, brain, feelings, digestive system, liver, heart, lungs, warm bed, food, roof, friends, the list goes on and on.

Take any of these away and you'd realise how grateful you would be to get them back.

When I see Sister Stan's incredible work, I feel very grateful that there are so many wonderful people like her in the world, beacons of the light, and hope, and true love.

Grá mór,
Damien Dempsey

Damien Dempsey is an Irish singer and songwriter who mixes traditional Irish folk with contemporary lyrics that deliver social and political commentaries on Irish society.

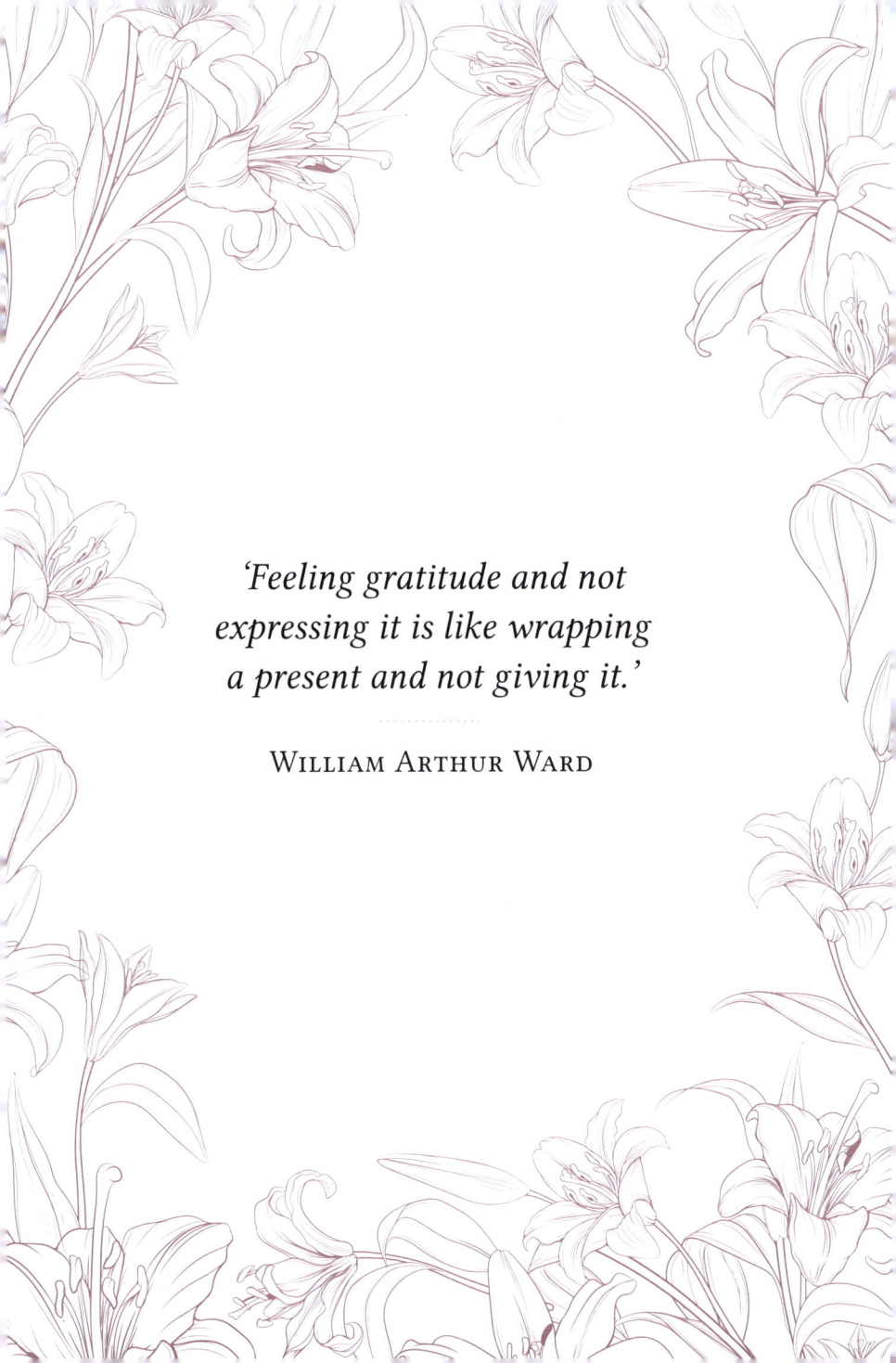

'Feeling gratitude and not expressing it is like wrapping a present and not giving it.'

WILLIAM ARTHUR WARD

THOSE WITH THE LEAST HAVE THE MOST GRATITUDE

Denis O'Brien

I grew up in a home where my father was the breadwinner and my mother the homemaker. She also had strong views on foreign policy and geopolitics.

My father, Dano, saw the world through a prism of business opportunities, while my mother, Iris, viewed it as one large family, where caring and sharing should take precedence over everything else. Her trenchant views about human rights and inequality meant that we, her children, often accompanied her on protests outside both the US and Russian embassies.

Today, Catherine, my wife, is the person who anchors our family of four young adult children. She also plays an active and important role in our businesses.

I am very grateful for the stability that a strong family brings and binds. Like most families, there are many moving parts in our daily lives – education, sports and my work schedule.

I have had an association with Haiti for over 20 years, and it reminds me of what Ireland was like after the Famine in the mid-19th century. Haitians have never had a break from pain and suffering. The demand by France for Haiti to pay 150 million francs – $19 billion in today's money – between 1804 and 1955 to buy its independence has bedevilled Haiti to this day.

It amazes me every time – I see more children smile in Haiti than I have ever seen anywhere else in the world. Why? I don't know, but I wonder is it that the smallest things bring the biggest joy? Is it the enthusiasm of knowledge imparted by a brilliant or thoughtful teacher? A bright vibrant classroom?

The world we share today with the impoverished without proper nourishment, the homeless, those who live under threat and so many uncertainties is a sad one. All the great advances that are being made in medicine and technology are being eclipsed by the shocking scale of inhumanity. Gaza is one the worst atrocities we have witnessed since the Second World War. Gaza and the genocide horrifies me, and the attack on Israeli citizens equally so, but there is no proportionality.

I often wonder are those with the least those who have the most gratitude.

When we talk about 'our world' what exactly do we mean? It is as much the world of the disadvantaged as it is that of the advantaged. In fact, I believe the disadvantaged should be prioritised over the rest of the world.

The world we occupy is spinning out of control with conflict, hyper-consumerism and the technologies that own and control us. Social media has become the 'digital fentanyl' for our children, with untold consequences.

Do we take gratitude for granted? Is it only when something goes wrong that we actually realise that we have had it so good?

I heard someone say: 'Forget about happiness, it is fleeting. Focus on being grateful.'

One of the great escapes for my father during his life was to head to the Wicklow mountains to run. I frequently joined him and, to this day, it is a special place, lost in nature in one of Ireland's natural treasures.

Although many years ago, I am still grateful.

As we all get older, I think we experience a greater sense of gratitude towards those who went before us, regretting that we didn't show more gratitude.

Hopefully, we can instil it in those coming after us.

....

Denis O'Brien is a native of Dublin. He was educated at UCD and Boston College. Married to Catherine, they have four children. He has business interests across a range of sectors in Ireland and internationally. He is involved in philanthropy, and is the founder of the Digicel Foundation, which has built schools and trained teachers across the Caribbean and in the South Pacific. He is the chairman and co-founder of Front Line Defenders, the International Foundation for the Protection of Human Rights Defenders, which is based in Dublin.

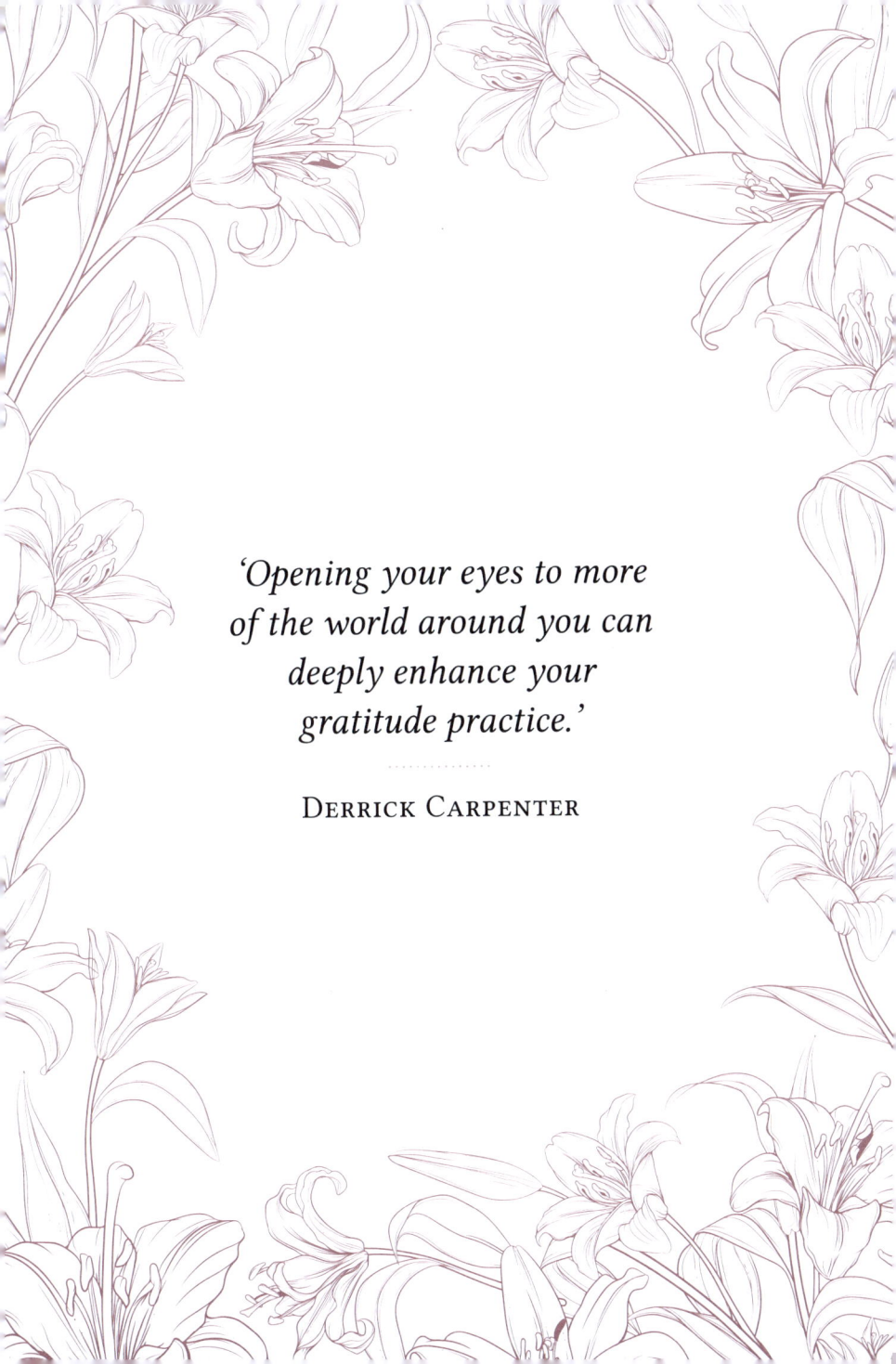

'Opening your eyes to more of the world around you can deeply enhance your gratitude practice.'

Derrick Carpenter

APPRECIATE WHAT YOU HAVE

Denise Charlton

As I look back, I realised, as children and teens, we were encouraged repeatedly to practise gratitude and appreciation. As I became increasingly aware of the deep inequalities around me, I came to appreciate all for which I had been encouraged to be grateful – grateful for a loving family, a home, access to education, opportunities for sport and access to nature.

Today, I really understand and appreciate education and the privilege of learning through school and university. I am grateful for the opportunity it gave me, translating into a career that I love. Every day, I feel grateful for a job that gives me purpose, an opportunity to work with great colleagues and others, responding to inequalities in Ireland and internationally.

Sport was central growing up, and whilst I never was good at it, it gave me an appreciation of exercise in life. The opportunity to swim in the sea regularly is something for which I am always grateful. It grounds me, stills me and sets me up for the day. Alone or with friends or with family, I am so grateful for the sea. As a very inadequate rower, I get to appreciate the sea further, and see areas of the country I love from a very different perspective. The methodical nature of the movement is calming and assuring. Hiking to the top of a mountain is where I go to regroup and ground myself, again grateful for so many opportunities to appreciate the physical exercise of the climb, and the often majestic and breathtaking scenery. In a world facing a massive biodiversity crisis, I am even more grateful for where we live and the opportunities for nature that I have.

After a recent health scare, I am grateful for the opportunity to heal and to appreciate good health again. Every day, I am grateful for good health and never take it for granted.

Finally, I am most grateful for family and friends, a wonderful partner and two gorgeous sons, parents who were and are generous in their love and presence, a brother and sister who are important friends in my life, and their partners and children who provide us with fun and adventures. For all of it, I am eternally grateful.

Denise Charlton is the chief executive of Community Foundation Ireland.

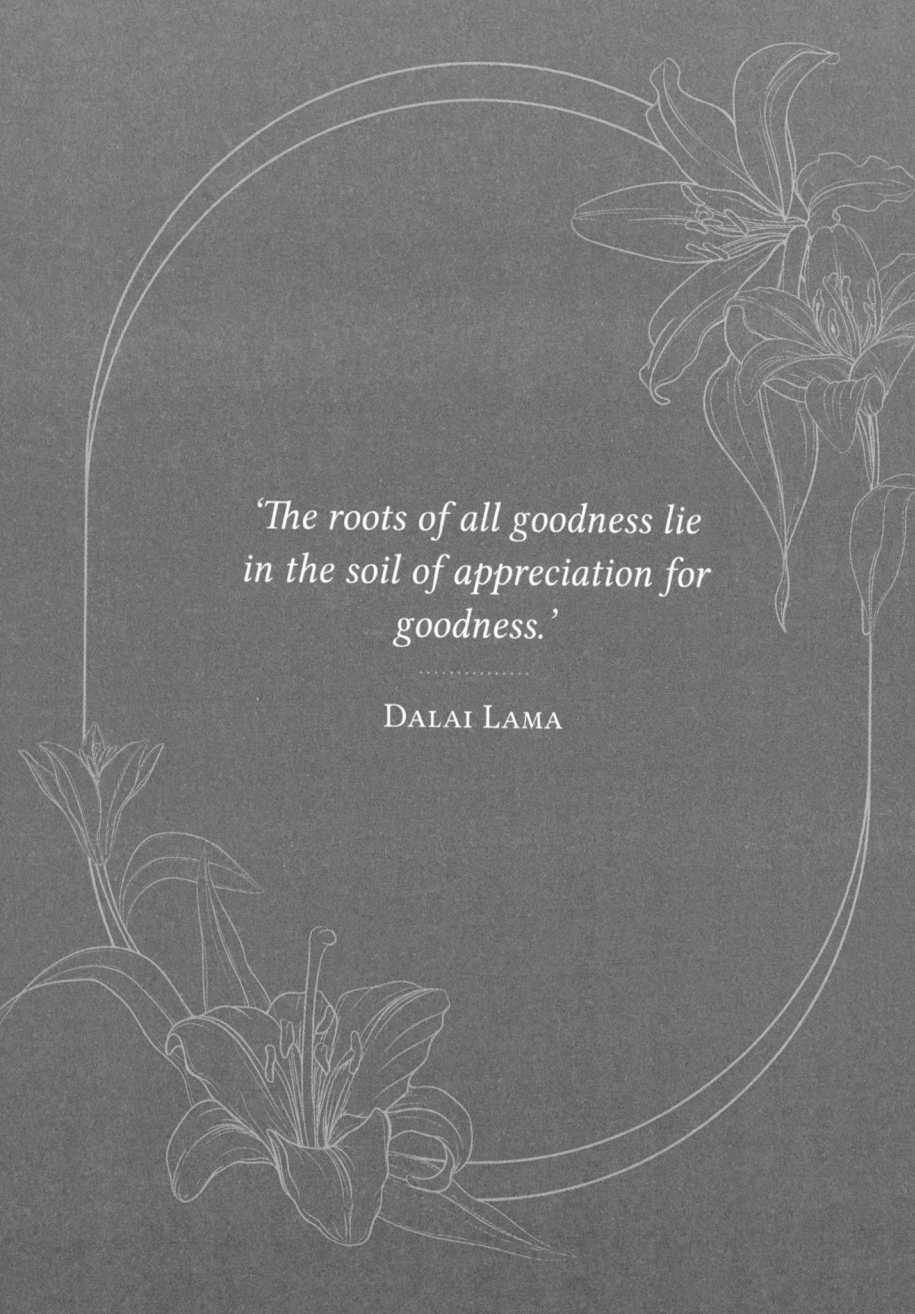

'The roots of all goodness lie in the soil of appreciation for goodness.'

DALAI LAMA

THE POWER OF PEACE

Derek Scally

Leaving the *Irish Times* office in central Berlin to cycle home, I am forever grateful for the peace.

Berlin is a remarkably flat city, so much so that my father once remarked to a mortified German woman he met soon after in Kerry: 'I suppose we have himself to thank for that.'

Himself – or rather the consequences of himself – loom large as I cycle westward through the Brandenburg Gate. It was here that the torchlit fascist parades passed 90 years ago, celebrating his rise to power. His hate-filled ideology becomes visible as I look left after the gate to see oblong, undulating concrete pillars remembering six million murdered European Jews.

I breathe easier once I've crossed the discreet line of cobbles in the road marking where, for 28 years, the Berlin Wall divided the capital.

Three wars – two hot, one cold – were launched from this city. Berlin's many ghosts remind us that peace is not a given.

That peace does seem like a given is thanks to the European Union, which has given Europe its longest-ever period of peace. The EU – easy to take for granted, mock or ignore – is something to be grateful for. Its Erasmus programme allowed me to study in

Berlin, opening a world to me where war was real and gratitude for peace palpable.

Arriving in my street, I often stop one door down from mine at the plaque to my former neighbour Erich Remarque. A century ago, after serving in the Imperial German army, he wrote here his novel *All Quiet on the Western Front*.

'To forget the horror is to become a part of it,' he warned. 'By remembering past horrors, we can strive to create a world where compassion, understanding and peace prevail.'

My cycle home leaves me with gratitude for living in this place where, for now at least, peace prevails.

Derek Scally is Berlin correspondent with the Irish Times *and author of* The Best Catholics in the World. *Based in Berlin since 2000, he is a regular contributor to German media outlets, including* Die Zeit *weekly newspaper and Deutschlandfunk radio.*

'*What separates privilege from entitlement is gratitude.*'

BRENE BROWN

CONNECTIONS AND COMMUNICATION

Diarmaid Ferriter

The impulse to retreat in troubled times is understandable, but the isolation such seclusion creates is damaging. Some years ago, Irish writer Mary Shine Thompson noted that for too many young people, their perceived safe spaces were 'shrinking, as they retire to the independent republics of their bedrooms – hermetically sealed personal spaces. Yet, the virtual space they can access through electronic means is expanding.' It is a troubling paradox, and many parents and educators have witnessed its consequences, especially in relation to increased anxiety and mental illness.

What I am most grateful for are the communication networks I am fortunate to have. These were born of a very different sense of interaction and social engagement in 1980s childhoods, and involved meeting, sharing and spending as much time as possible outside of home. I am not romanticising these childhoods, as each generation faces its own struggles, and there were many social and economic problems during that era, but the bonds we established then have endured and provide much comfort, sharing and laughter; a bedrock of continuity and familiarity. Sharing dilutes angst and provides levity and perspective.

Teenagers are always self-conscious, no matter what era they are living through, but we were not bombarded to the same extent as now with images and messages of how we *should* be. We did not discover things in the artificial way that today creates so many pressures and unreal expectations. We sometimes wrote letters to each other, some of which I still have, and they reveal all the embarrassing preoccupations and notions we carried in our youthful, sometimes messed up minds. But they also document some of our healthy passions, and that we put them down in such an intimate and durable form was also a measure of something deeper and more lasting that we carried into adulthood. I am very grateful for those connections and shared pasts that make for current comfort blankets of friendship that will remain wrapped around us as we deal with ageing, and help buffet us against the winds of contemporary woes.

Diarmaid Ferriter is Professor of Modern Irish History at UCD.

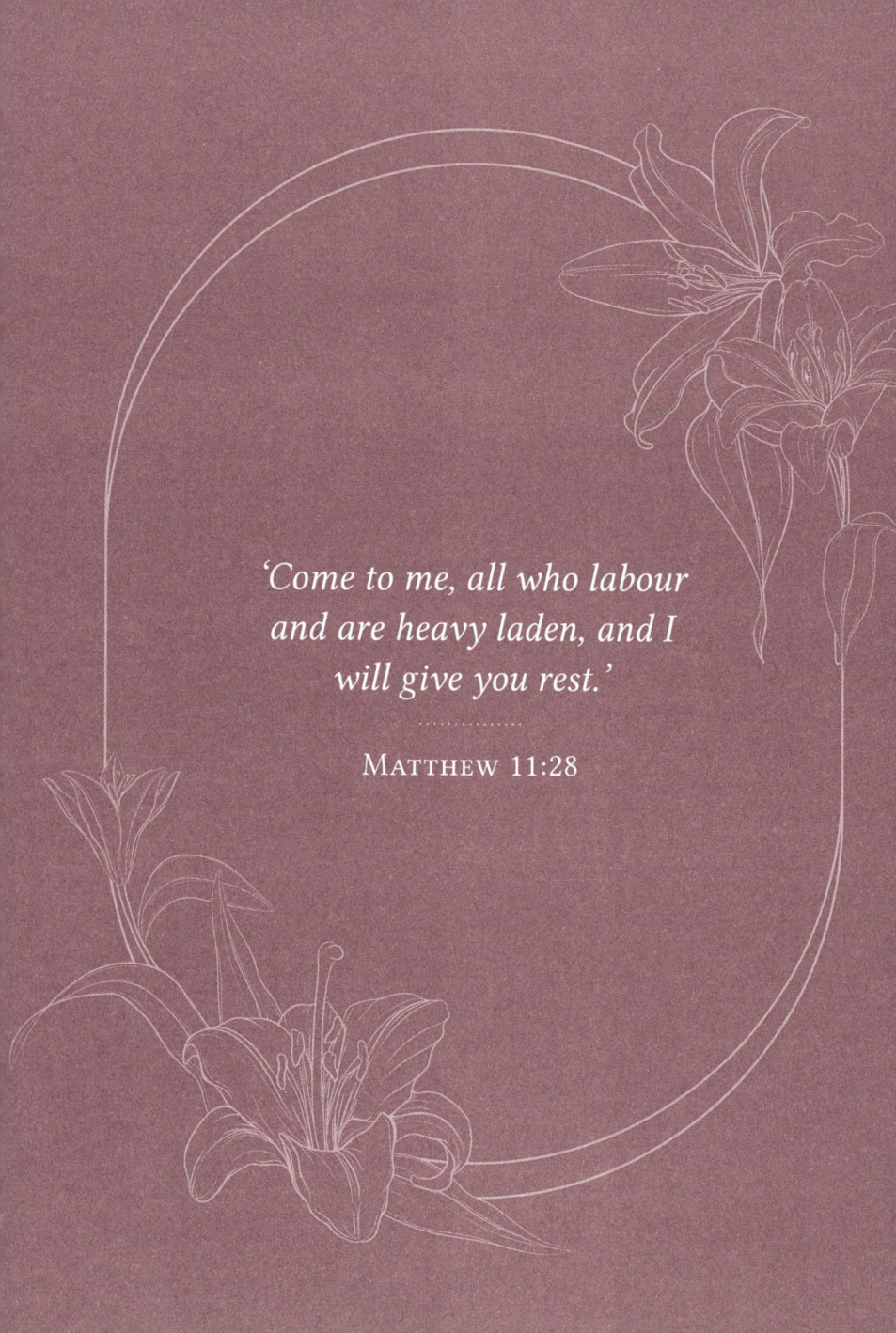

'Come to me, all who labour and are heavy laden, and I will give you rest.'

Matthew 11:28

· GRATITUDE ·

ANOTHER DAY IN PARADISE

Eddie Gilmore

The first time I walked on the Camino to Santiago de Compostela, I was with an Australian friend called James. He had brought with him a stove and a billycan (that's quite usual in the outback apparently!), and we developed a bit of a reputation for, amongst other things, being the two guys who would stop at random places to make tea. We would also sing a few psalms and we would marvel at the stunning landscapes we were passing through.

Early one morning, we were on a bench outside a pilgrim hostel waiting for the water in the billy to boil for our tea. The birds were starting to sing, there was the pleasant sound of rushing water from the river nearby, and the sun was rising above the trees. We were sitting there in companionable silence and then James said, 'Another day in paradise'.

These words inspired both a song and the title of a book. They also helped me to try to enter each new day in a particular way. When I got home from the Camino, I said to myself every morning as I got out of bed and opened the curtains, 'Another day in paradise'. It was late spring/early summer, and it was perhaps easier then to say it. I had also returned from that first stint on the Camino with a heart that had been filled with goodness and gratitude. It wore off a bit with the passing weeks and months. As the seasons changed and as the usual worries of life came back, it was not so easy to say those words. But still, from time to time, I recall sitting on that bench outside a pilgrim hostel in Spain and those words of James, and I try to say thank you for another day in paradise.

* * *

Eddie Gilmore grew up in an Irish family in Coventry and was later part of the L'Arche community in Canterbury for twenty-eight years, and it's where he met his wife, Yim Soon. After seven years as CEO of a London-based charity called the Irish Chaplaincy, he moved to Kilkenny to be leader/CEO of L'Arche Ireland. Another Day in Paradise *is the title of his third book.*

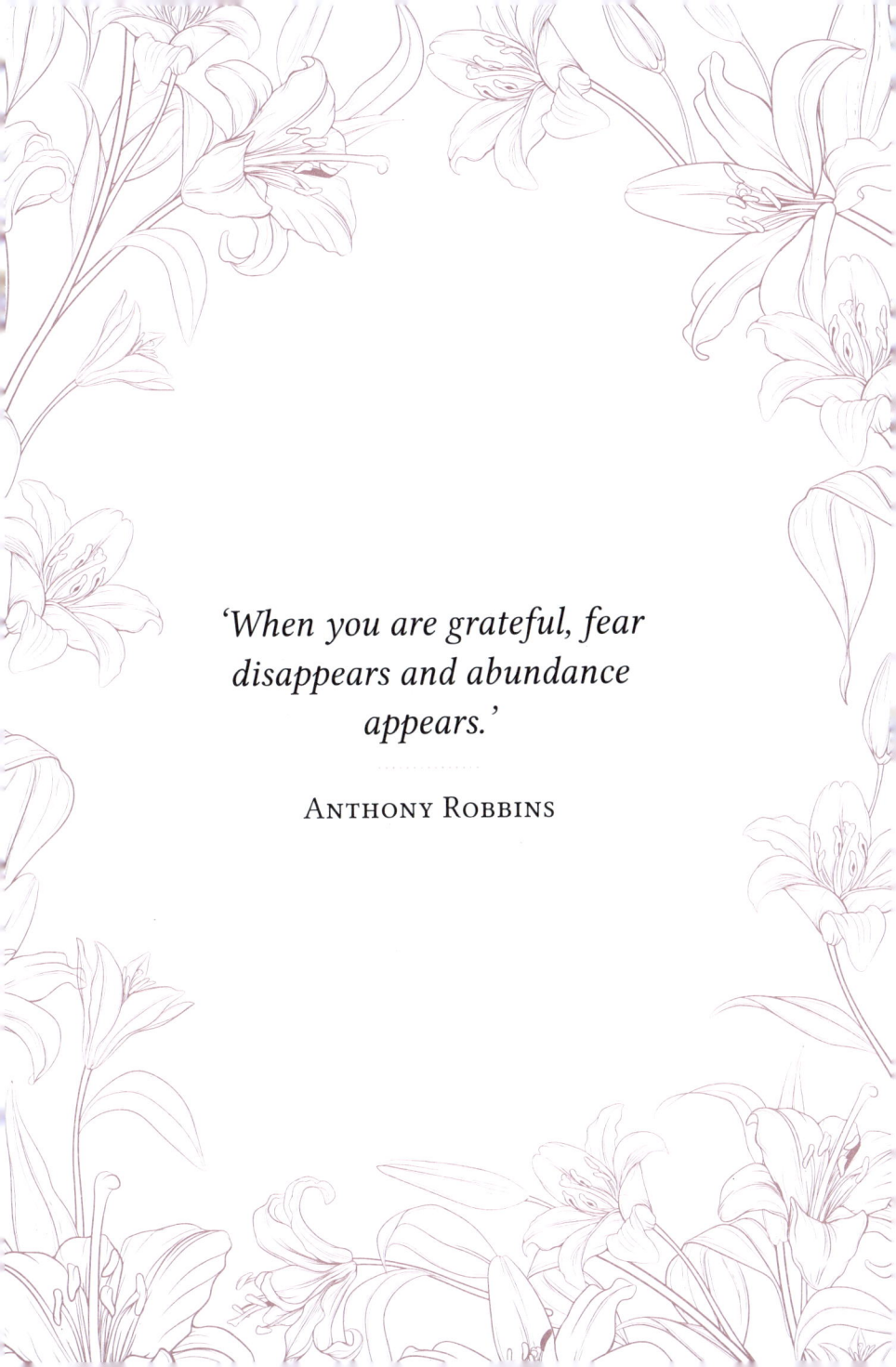

'When you are grateful, fear disappears and abundance appears.'

ANTHONY ROBBINS

HOPE

Edith Cunningham

I used to hate hearing about gratitude. 'Be grateful' sounded like an insurmountable task when feeling at your lowest. When you can see the world on fire, it is hard to be grateful. But when we forget to acknowledge the beauty around us, the little things that make human existence great, we become numb, desensitised and incapable of sharing kindness with ourselves and others, which is beneficial to no one.

To me, gratitude is the simple privileges that often get overlooked, the breeze in the trees, laughing with loved ones, looking at my dog's ears bouncing on a walk. Gratitude is recognising how lucky I am to have the support systems I do. Gratitude is feeling the range of human emotions and experiences, even if uncomfortable; it is an honour to be alive.

When feeling grateful feels like a foreign, unfamiliar feeling that leaves me seeing everything shrouded in a cloud of numbness, I try to remember the 'immediates' – the feeling in my hands, the ability to get up and move around, singing one of my favourite songs, reading a great book or watching a funny comfort film with loved ones.

Gratitude is also remembering I'm not perfect, the world isn't perfect and nothing is or should be perfect. Perfection is boring, sterile and an impossibility. Being human is to be flawed. Gratitude isn't about comparison, 'oh this person has it better or worse than me, so I should or shouldn't be happy about this' – this helps no one and isolates us further.

Gratitude is having hope, hope in myself, in others and in the world. Hope for a better, more equal, sustainable, supportive, kinder world. Hope combined with meaningful action is how we create change.

....
Edie Cunningham, 26, is a charity worker in Dublin.

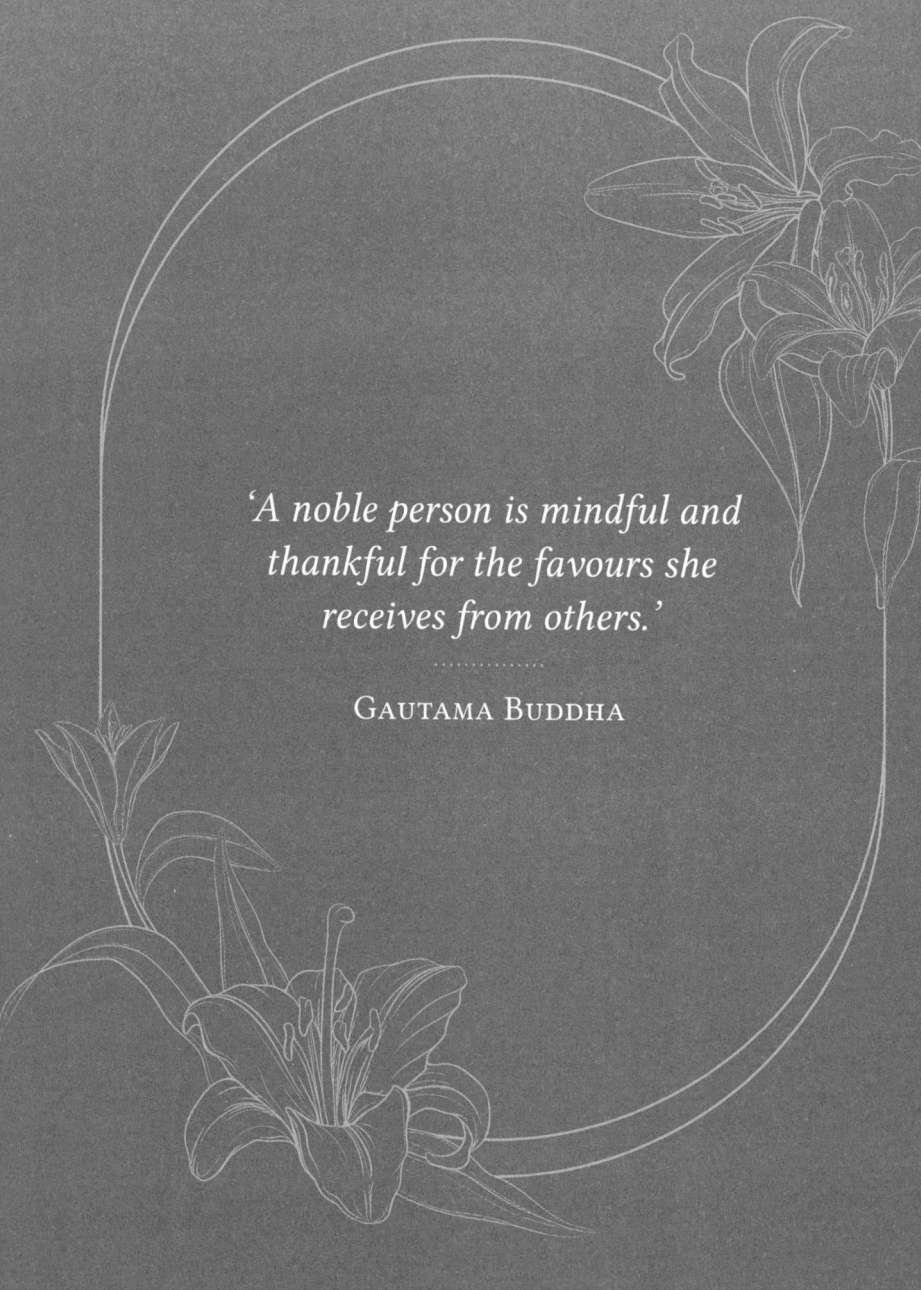

'*A noble person is mindful and thankful for the favours she receives from others.*'

GAUTAMA BUDDHA

· GRATITUDE ·

CHERISH THE BLESSINGS IN OUR LIVES

Ellen O'Malley-Dunlop

In our ordinary everyday lives we can take so much for granted. It is when that default position of taking things for granted is disrupted that feelings of gratitude get triggered. For example, if I think of people living in the many parts of the world today that are being torn apart by war or who are suffering from famine, I immediately feel grateful for the life and the choices that I have; that I live in a democracy, that I can vote and that I can raise my voice to advocate for change without fear that I'll be punished for doing so. Of course, life is not perfect, and we still have some way to go to have equal rights for everyone, but I am grateful for having the opportunities that afford me to have these choices and to speak out.

Gratitude for family and the kindness and compassion of others is a reminder to cherish the blessings in our lives, and to be grateful for the love and support that surrounds us. It is a reminder to be present in the moment and to appreciate the simple joys that life brings.

On a personal note, I am grateful for all that I have learned from the huge shame and pain I felt for many years because of a failed first marriage when I was 18, and which lasted only two years. It gave me first-hand experience and insight into the unacceptable injustices that existed in 1970s' and 1980s' Ireland for single parents, and spurred me on to do all I could to challenge the inequalities and the harmful stereotypes and biases that limit women's potential in our society. It also introduced me to the world of therapy, which had a profound and positive effect on my life, and enabled me to trust again and enjoy the love of a good man who is the father of our four sons, grandfather of our eight grandchildren and my husband of 43 years.

As I reflect on what gratitude means in today's world, I realise how important an emotion it is, particularly during these times of great uncertainty and disturbance. Feelings of gratitude can affirm that there are good things in the world, and can go a long way to keeping hope alive.

* *

Ellen O'Malley-Dunlop served as CEO for the Dublin Rape Crisis Centre for ten years. As a result of this role, she has become a highly respected advocate for the rights of victims of sexual violence in this jurisdiction. Ellen was elected as chair of the board of the National Women's Council of Ireland in 2017.

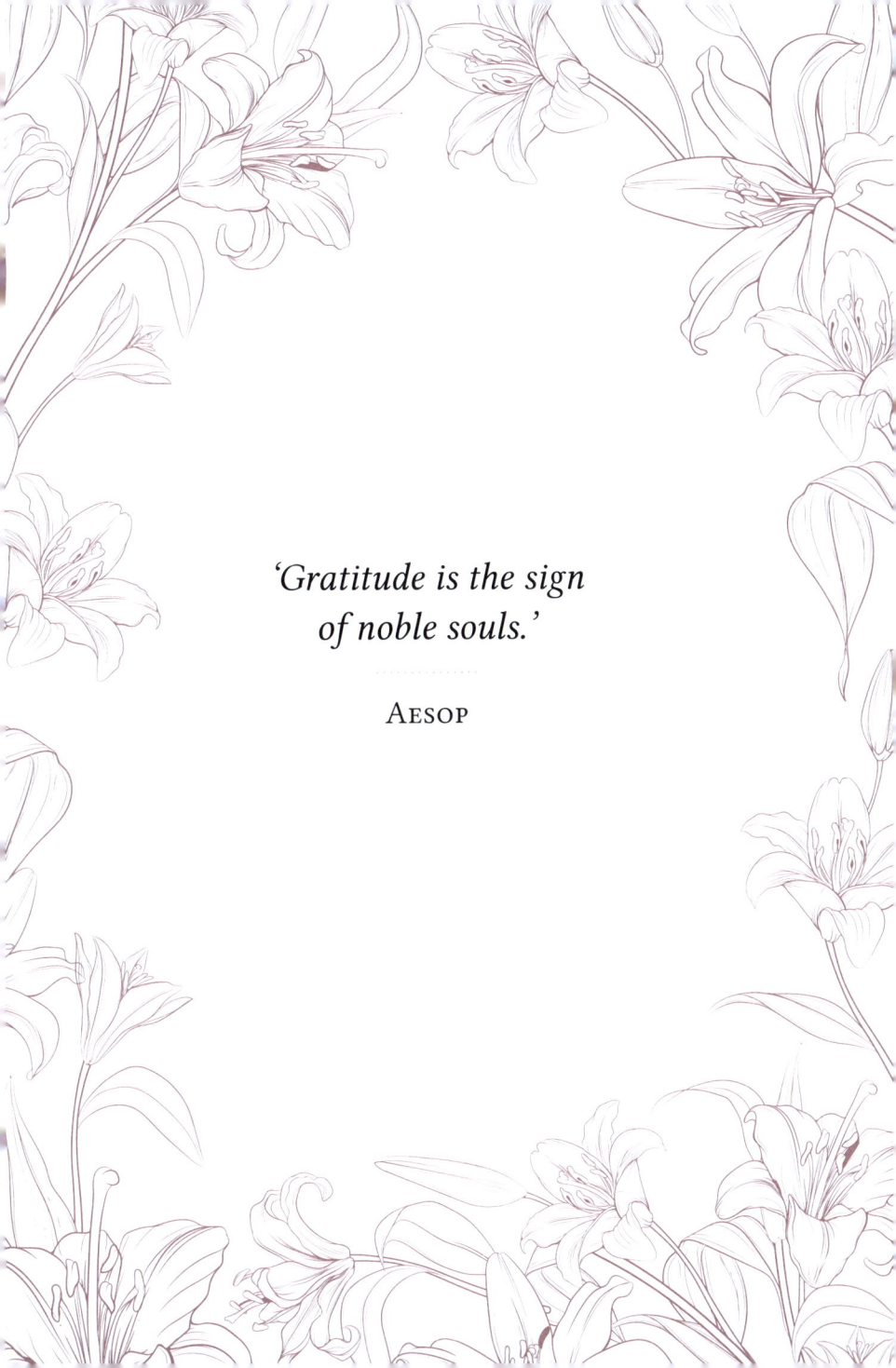

'Gratitude is the sign
of noble souls.'

Aesop

CONVERTING A GRATITUDE SCEPTIC

Emily Logan

It's fair to say I was a 'gratitude sceptic' until my mother died on New Year's morning in 2011. At her request, we had looked after her at home up until the night before she died, when she was admitted to a hospice. Some months later, I was on a train on my way back to Dublin from Belfast. I was knee-deep in the emotional and physical effects of grief, a grief I couldn't express openly at work. The phone rang and it was Anna from the hospice. Anna listened and then shared a simple exercise in gratitude that she felt might assist me: to write, at night before bed, three things for which I was grateful. I didn't think I could do it, as joy had temporarily left my life and I didn't feel grateful for anything. As the days passed, my trust in Anna allowed me to relax about the process and gradually observe things I could put on such a list. It did help.

Why was I a 'gratitude sceptic'? It derived from my years of working in frontline services with children and families, where I often observed people almost being made to feel grateful about the less than adequate support they had received. I could see people in fear of questioning authority because they feared losing any

· GRATITUDE ·

support, no matter how poor it was. I can see this also now in those in the international protection system.

I have, over the years, continued to use Anna's simple exercise when I'm bothered by something. I simply write on my phone, sometimes it might be one thing during the day if I'm busy. This simple, private acknowledgement of things to be grateful for keeps a form of balance in my life.

Thank you, Anna.

> ....
> *Emily Logan is best known as Ireland's first Ombudsman for Children. She subsequently served as chief commissioner of the Irish Human Rights and Equality Commission, and is now a commissioner in the Garda Síochána Ombudsman Commission.*

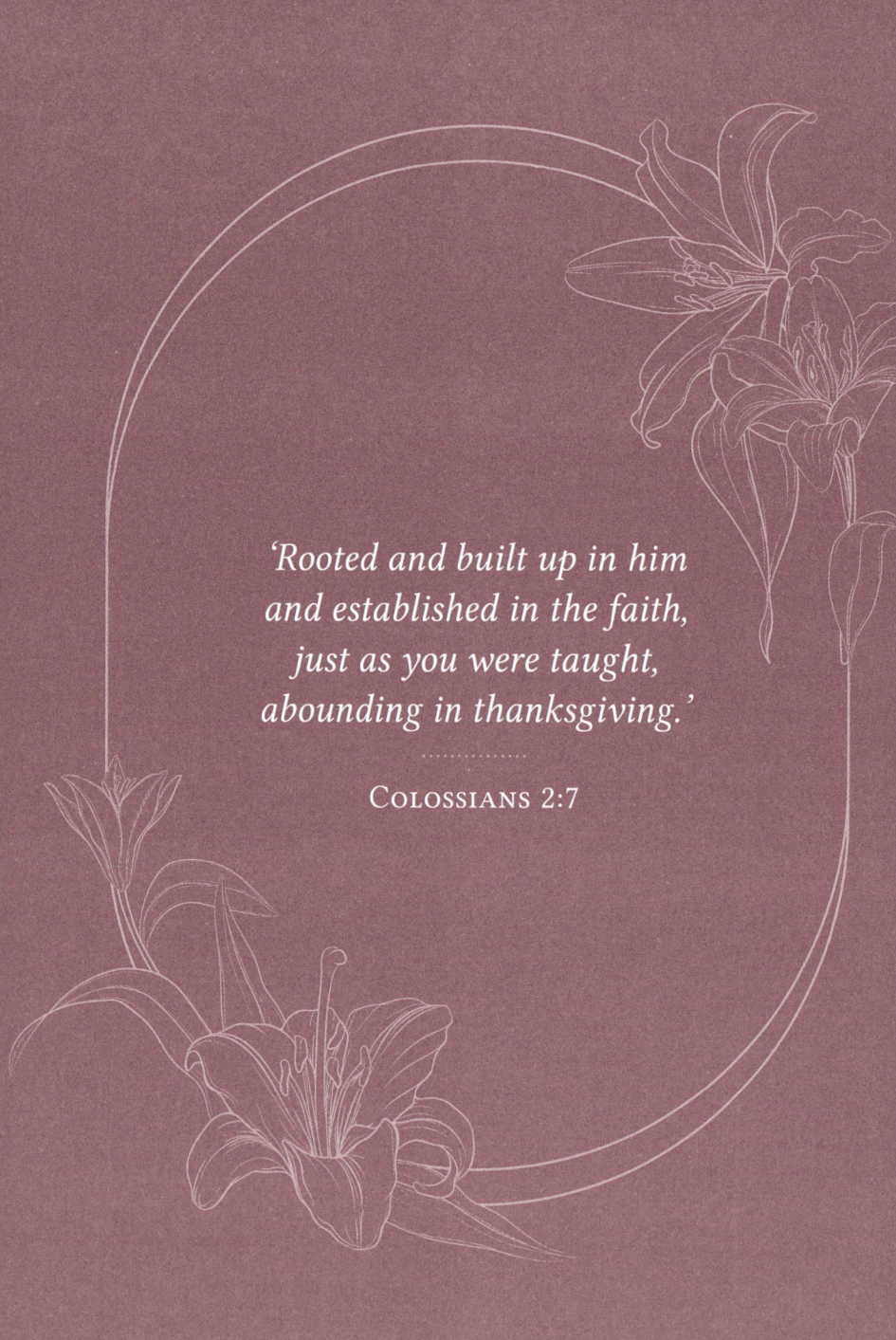

'Rooted and built up in him and established in the faith, just as you were taught, abounding in thanksgiving.'

Colossians 2:7

· GRATITUDE ·

THE ROCKY ROAD TO GRATITUDE

Emily Quinn

Gratitude: To begin with, I've so much to be grateful for, and I'm thankful for it all on a daily basis. I am grateful for my family – my husband, who loves and encourages me to be a better person daily, and for the children we have together, who bring me so much joy and laughter. Grateful to still have my mother alongside me. I call her daily, mostly with life questions – she always had a good answer, always grateful for my Momma. Grateful for a roof over my head, serenity in my life, a job I adore, friends who I laugh and cry with – weekly probably. Peace on our streets in a lovely community. Grateful for art, music, books, film, all I'm still learning about.

But mostly, I am grateful to be right here, right now, today! It's been, at times, a rocky road to get here – life has thrown in some curveballs along the way. But I am grateful to be here at this very moment, and yet every single thing I've done, and every choice I've made previously, has led me to where I am right now. I know it seems very obvious, but sometimes to reflect on where you've been is a very profound viewpoint – and I am grateful now I can see why some decisions were made to get me to this exact spot. I have especially felt gratitude for the last year ... the last year has been a massive learning curve, learning about people and humanity and empathy has been the most challenging. Yet, I am grateful to have so many wonderful people by my side; some pals didn't make it to today, so to reflect on this from time to time makes today a lovely place to be – a place full of gratitude.

. . . .

Emily Quinn is a photographer based in Dublin. She lives with her husband, Niall, their two children, Dylan and Euan, and their dog, Sophie.

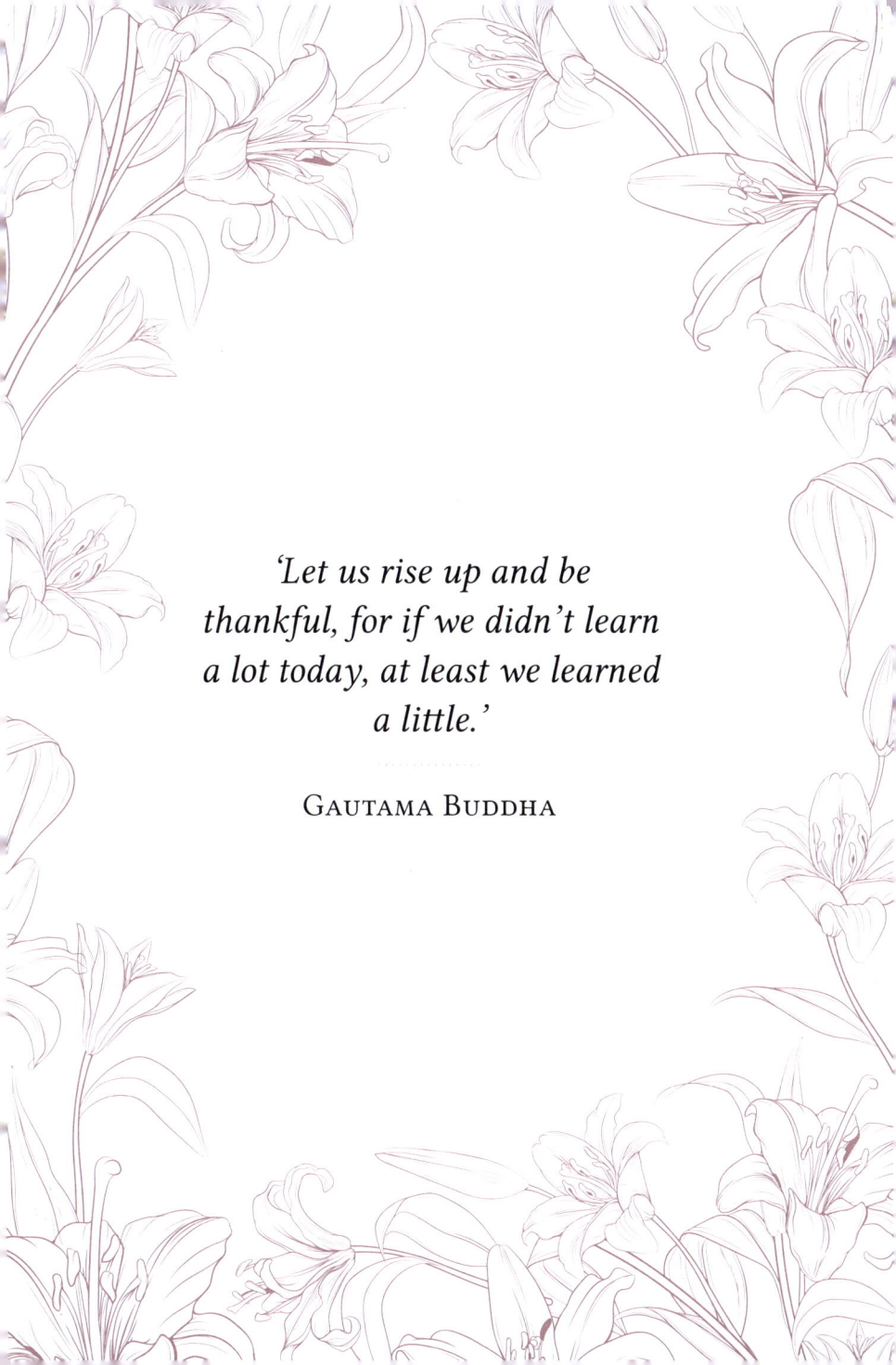

'Let us rise up and be thankful, for if we didn't learn a lot today, at least we learned a little.'

Gautama Buddha

THE TRANSFER OF TRUST

Enda Kenny

Politicians, if elected, should understand gratitude. I felt it each time a returning officer called my name and uttered the words 'deemed to be elected', officially recognising the transfer of trust and responsibility to the public representative to work in the interests and service of the people. I kept that trust as the foundation of my politics over many years.

I recall my gratitude to the Ethiopian taxi driver in Chicago who travelled back 15 miles to return my mobile phone, maybe because I asked about his family circumstances in Eritrea.

I recall my gratitude to my fellow cyclists who pulled me from a deep drain when my bike skidded on a wet surface during a Pink Ribbon Charity cycle for cancer research.

I recall my gratitude to my Maker when I turned to face east at 18,000 ft on Kilimanjaro, to see and appreciate a molten sun climbing rapidly into a blue sky and seemingly so close to almost touch it.

I recall my unbridled joy and gratitude at the birth of our three wonderful, healthy children.

Gratitude brings about a feeling of something deeper than mere thanks.

It comes in many forms. Just like cancer.

· GRATITUDE ·

For me, life became a time of blood tests, scans, MRIs, conversations and then assessment and determination. Malignant.

Everybody faces mortality in their own way. It's a sobering thought. Time suddenly becomes so critical, and we never know how much we have.

Will I ever walk in the door at home again, have a glass of wine with my wife, or a pint with friends, or go and see a football match in MacHale Park? Will I ever get the chance to finish the book I was reading?

Questions flood your mind. The same applies to everybody, and some unfortunately do not get that time. Attitude becomes so important. Just before the anaesthetic is delivered, you realise that you place the next stage of your life in the hands of people you do not know, have never met and have to rely on their skill, experience and medical expertise.

So now, having less tomorrows than yesterdays, I have engaged in all the therapies and other treatments in setting out on this next stage of my life. I do so without fear, having had a clear run so far!

Cancer survivors have a closeness and a bond in telling their stories of courage and in dealing with new situations.

For me, I have a newer and deeper appreciation of the things that really are important – love of family, understanding and respect of neighbours and friends, how complex and fragile life actually is. But I also understand that despite the world's many serious challenges, life is there to be lived and to contribute to on the planet that we call home.

It's not about fixating on what you want, but appreciation of what you have.

That's where my focus is now, especially in helping the Cancer Fund for Children, where families cope with the shock of having a child diagnosed with cancer.

For that, and to the Ultimate Referee who has ordained that I can still continue to face the future in good health, I can truthfully say that I now have the deepest understanding of the meaning of that single word. Gratitude.

· ·

Enda Kenny is married to Fionnuala and they have three grown-up children. He began his career as a teacher. He was elected to Dáil Éireann in 1975, served as Taoiseach between 2011 and 2017, and retired from active politics in 2020.

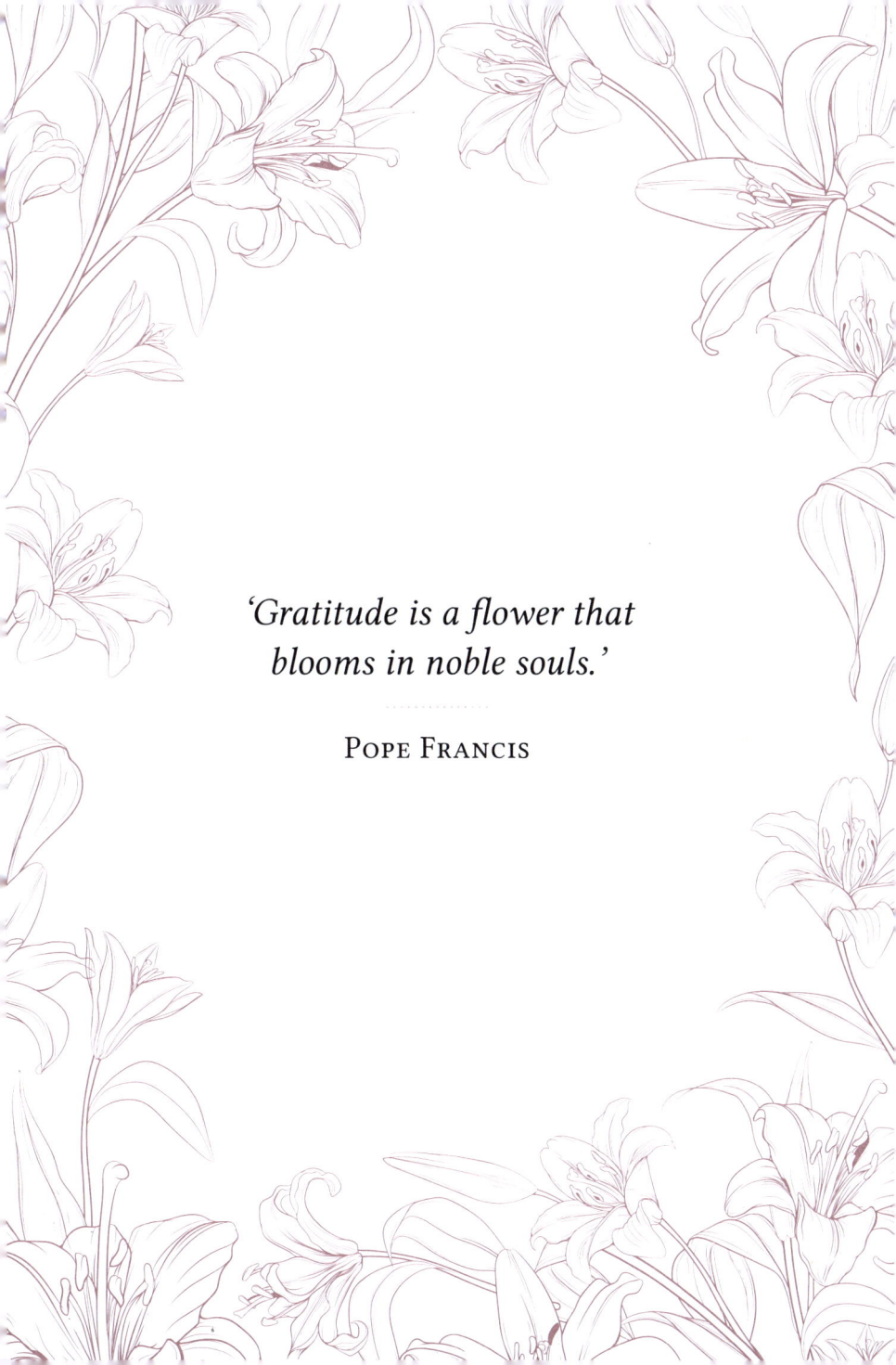

'Gratitude is a flower that
blooms in noble souls.'

Pope Francis

THE FAMILY GLUE

Fiona Looney

One of the most widely disseminated myths about motherhood is that you can't be your child's parent and their friend. You can, and I have. When my children were very small, I got on the floor and joined them in their wildly creative imaginary worlds, populating them with vivid characters and creatures. Later, we sat in the stands and cheered for the same football teams, I read the books they did so we could critique them together, we raved about theatre productions and music gigs we'd seen together. Now that they're young adults, we still cheer and read and rave, but now we socialise together afterwards as well. I don't share all their parties and pints – nor they mine – but there are enough of them to remind me that after love, laughter is the glue that holds our family together.

Only part of that was planned. It was my idea to become these three amazing people's mother. They didn't plan that. They didn't choose me as a parent.

But they did choose me as their friend, and that has been the single greatest honour of my life. I give thanks for it in every moment we share together.

Fiona Looney, mother (and friend) of Ciara, Cian and Uainín, is a columnist, playwright and scriptwriter.

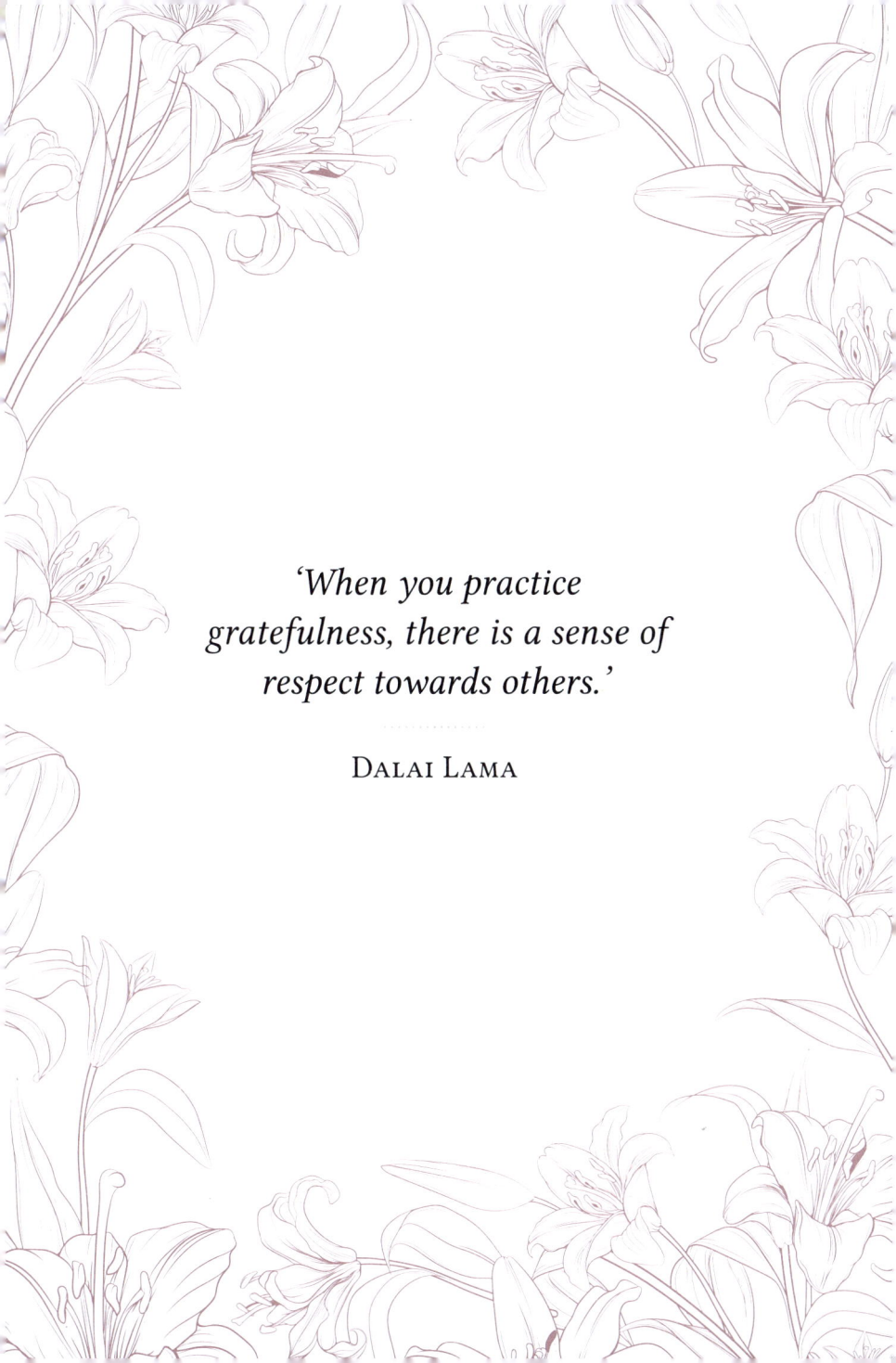

'When you practice gratefulness, there is a sense of respect towards others.'

DALAI LAMA

· SR STAN ·

OPENING UP

Frances Fitzgerald

Gratitude, to me, embodies a deep sense of thankfulness for the opportunities and choices that I have experienced in my life.

I have always felt eternally grateful for the opportunities the Irish state gave to my family, and in particular to my father. As a young man, he entered the army, which created a prosperous life for my family, and in turn led to opportunities for me and my siblings. He did not come from a privileged background, and constantly reminded me to be thankful for a state that opened up to provide for all – this is a memory firmly etched in my mind.

Being a mother to three boys has been a big part of my life. I have a deep appreciation for the joy they have brought to my life. I'm very conscious of the range of issues that face parents. Gratitude comes to mind when you know your children are living healthy and happy lives.

I'm also grateful for being part of a modern Ireland that opened up dramatically for women, for the LGBTI+ community, and for those who were previously excluded.

As a politician and social worker, I have had the unique opportunity to play a role in shaping modern Ireland. I am thankful for the work I got an opportunity to complete as a minister –

guiding two historic referendums through the Oireachtas, and for initiating progressive legislation as Minister for Justice.

I have always been humbled to receive the trust of the electorate to represent them at local, national and European level. There is nothing more heartening than for people to go out and voice support for your work.

Practising gratitude has enhanced my resilience and enriched my relationships.

....

Frances Fitzgerald is a former MEP for Dublin, former Tánaiste and minister, serving in three different portfolios. Prior to entering politics, Frances served as chair of the National Women's Council of Ireland, and worked as a social worker in both London and Dublin. Frances lives with her husband in Castleknock, where she raised her three sons.

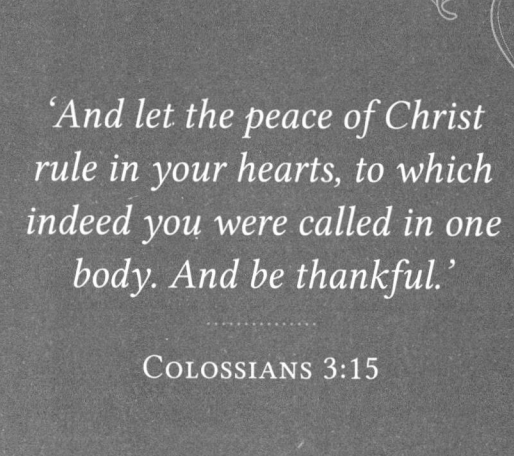

'And let the peace of Christ rule in your hearts, to which indeed you were called in one body. And be thankful.'

COLOSSIANS 3:15

· GRATITUDE ·

DAILY DOSE OF WELL-BEING

Frances Ruane

Sr Stan's invitation to reflect on what I feel grateful for in my daily life is timely – a reminder that when we dwell on the positive, we feel so much better about ourselves and about everyone else, especially our families, friends and neighbours.

Nature gives us all a generous daily dose of well-being when we let it. Even on the wettest winter days, there is pleasure to be found in the changing clouds, the damp trees and the dripping hedges. For me, the people and buildings around me are also a source of nurture and energy – something I was much less aware of before Covid.

As a (mostly) Dublin native, my life is enriched by Dublin's population becoming more diverse with every year. The sounds of so many languages in my own neighbourhood remind me on a daily basis that our 'local' is part of a global humanity, where many do not have our good fortune and deserve our support. I would love to see us getting more comfortable talking about our personal, cultural, political and social values.

I do love how most Irish people engage positively with each other on the street, at work, in the shops or wherever. We must keep this if we are to remain a welcoming people. It lifts my spirits to hear foreigners in Dublin adopting the Irish habit of saying 'thank you' to the bus driver on exiting the bus. I have had a rich life so far, and have been personally blessed with many opportunities to give 'public service' over my lifetime. The rewards of these opportunities far outweigh the frustrations that policy changes are slow, leaving human needs unmet for too long. It has been a pleasure to be reminded of how much I have to be grateful for.

••••••••••••••••••••••••••••••••••

Frances Ruane is an economist who taught at TCD for 30 years before becoming director of the ESRI. She has contributed to many government reports over the past 30 years in areas from education, health and taxation to social welfare, disability, legal aid and spatial planning.

'The root of joy
is gratefulness.'

David Steindl-Rast

THE CALL OF THE SEA

Fran McNulty

I mostly feel gratitude for the sea. As a Midlander, I have always craved the ocean. Summers as a child were always spent in Enniscrone, in my father's native County Sligo, one of the most beautiful beaches on the west coast. I feel gratitude for the memories made in the dunes along the seafront, memories with my late brother Gary, for whom Enniscrone meant freedom. My craving for the sea first became apparent to me in my late teens, as a student travelling daily on the DART along the seafront. The sea would change every day and was a marvel to me. I have fed that craving as often as possible. I am lucky enough to be able to spend free time walking the beaches of Mayo and Sligo, swimming in cold, crisp, refreshing waters, or paddling through calm waters on a summer's day, insulated from reality, enjoying the simplicity of nature.

That connection with nature I feel is probably best expressed by the poet Máirtín Ó Direáin in his poem 'Buíochas', translated to 'Gratitude' in his collection *Tacar Dánta*.

*It's time I made my gratitude
Known to you, you elements
That I repaid your help,
You bare crags,
You foaming Seas
That used to lave
My cheeks so gently
When I had none to confide in
None who would bear my burden
And open wisdom's door.
Inside the enchanted castle to save me
When the force of the dark will
Surged towards me.*

I feel gratitude for music too. Music that can lift my spirits when I am down, or chime with something I am experiencing in life. Often the most surprising of artists can resonate with me. I find that music can also take me back in time, to relive an experience or a feeling. That is sometimes a good thing, but other times a bad thing!

I also feel gratitude for my health. I never take it for granted. Most of all, I feel gratitude for my family and friends. Through life's challenges you begin to learn who you can count on most. Those closest don't judge, or want; they are just there, to love and guide and spend time together. The bond we have with the humans we love is surely the greatest thing in life; for that, I feel immense gratitude.

Fran presents Prime Time *on RTÉ television. He has worked with the national broadcaster for almost twenty years, presenting television and radio programmes and working as an investigative journalist. Fran was also a news correspondent with RTÉ News. A native of County Longford, he lives in Dublin.*

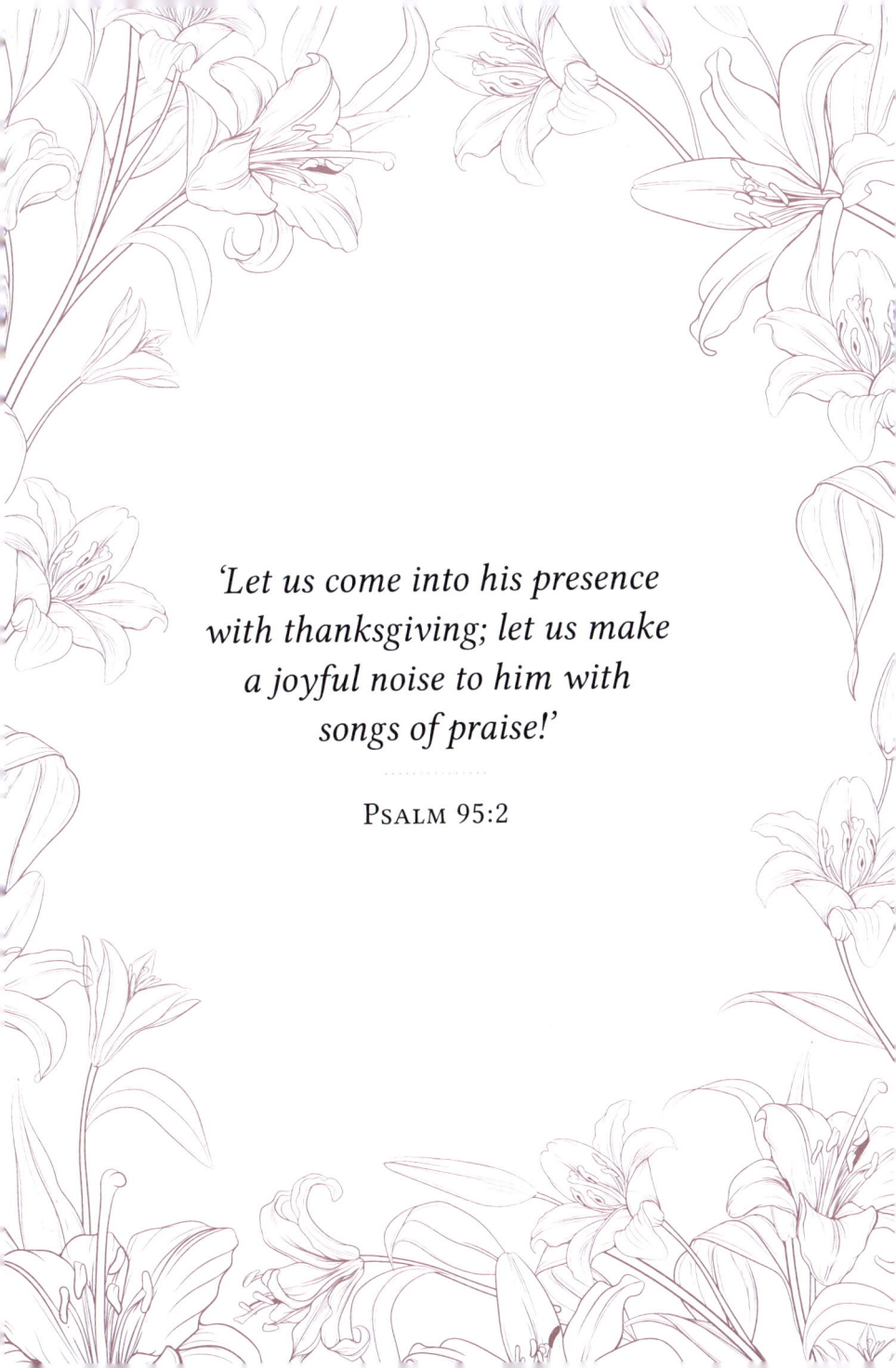

'Let us come into his presence with thanksgiving; let us make a joyful noise to him with songs of praise!'

Psalm 95:2

MAYBE, JUST MAYBE!

Gary Mason

As someone with a calling to work in the area of conflict transformation, peacebuilding and the role of religion in the public square, is it possible to be grateful? In looking back on my life, having lived through almost 30 years of an internal civil war on this island, and 25 years of a stop-start peace process, am I grateful for life and living? The answer is a categorical 'Yes!'

I've spent, by choice, 35 years plus of my life as a clergy person, in some of the toughest, most conflict-ridden areas of Belfast, and the last ten years of my life leading an organisation, Rethinking Conflict, in the area of conflict transformation. Currently, I am working in three areas, namely my own Irish context, the Israeli-Palestinian theatre and the United States. To many people working in those areas, it could be a recipe for despair and melancholy, not gratitude!

Yet, I'm deeply grateful for people I meet every day, who get out of bed, sometimes facing very difficult, perplexing situations, realising that the small contributions in life are the ones that ultimately make a difference. I've seen colleagues, even in the midst of the polarisation in the United States at the moment, see the humanity and the image of God in another person, even though politically they may not always see eye to eye. And as we despair about the Middle Eastern crisis, and wonder if there will ever be a solution, I'm grateful for daily conversations at the moment with both Palestinians and Israelis who refuse to give up in the midst of a bloody war. There are so many individuals looking for ways forward in very perplexing and difficult situations, and every day when I get up in my home city of Belfast, which has been transformed by our peace process, I am grateful.

I have hosted over one thousand Palestinians and Israelis in Belfast and Dublin over the last ten years, looking at lessons from our Irish peace process.

On one occasion, when a group of Israelis and Palestinians arrived in Belfast, a young Palestinian woman came up and said to me, 'Gary, I think this is just a waste of time.' In replying to this young woman, I said, 'You may well be right, it may be a waste of time, but at the end of the week, I hope you can just say three words to me.' She naturally asked, 'What three words would those be?' I replied, 'Maybe, just maybe!' That maybe at the end of this week, with some of the lessons from the Irish peace process, that maybe you can return to your region breathing the oxygen of hope.

The evening before the delegation travelled back to that fractured region of the Middle East, that young Palestinian woman came up to me with tears in her eyes and said three words: 'Maybe, just maybe.' I'm grateful for the lessons of our peace process, as maybe that region of the Middle East, which holds a place deep within my heart, that *maybe, just maybe*, someday they will be grateful for a completely new beginning.

> The Rev. Dr Gary Mason is a Methodist minister who founded and directs the Belfast-based conflict transformation nonprofit organisation, Rethinking Conflict.

'But thanks be to God, who in Christ always leads us in triumphal procession, and through us spreads the fragrance of the knowledge of him everywhere.'

2 CORINTHIANS 2:14

· GRATITUDE ·

GIVING BACK

Gemma Hoole

I am so grateful for where my life has gone from eight years ago when I was pregnant and homeless, living in a tent on the streets. Then, when I was six months pregnant, I was given a chance as a lovely lady offered me a room to stay in at her home. Then, when my son was six months old, I got my forever home with Focus Ireland. I'm so grateful to wake up every morning with my son in our forever home.

My housing officer got me into the PETE (Preparation for Education Training and Employment) education and creative arts project. There I started doing courses and ended up designing two gardens. Both ended up in the newspapers. One of the gardens is called Gem Moon; it's in my estate.

I am so grateful to be able to give back in life as now I've become a peer support worker with Focus Ireland to support people in homelessness.

I cycle into work every day with a smile on my face. If I can give hope to someone who is going though homelessness and let them know it won't always be like this, or support someone who has been homeless, that's made my day.

Eight years ago I never thought I'd be where I am today. It just shows that giving someone a chance can change their whole life. If it was not for Focus Ireland I wouldn't have had all the opportunities I have had.

> Gemma Hoole is a peer support worker in Focus Ireland's southeast services. She currently lives in a Focus Housing Association property with her eight-year-old son, Emanuel. Gemma chose to work as a peer support worker as she has experienced homelessness and wants to support other people who are currently experiencing this. Gemma loves exercising. She cycles to work every day, works out and lifts weights, which she says really helps her mental health. Gemma has experience in garden design and recently completed the stunning Gem Moon garden in Waterford, which was launched in summer 2023.

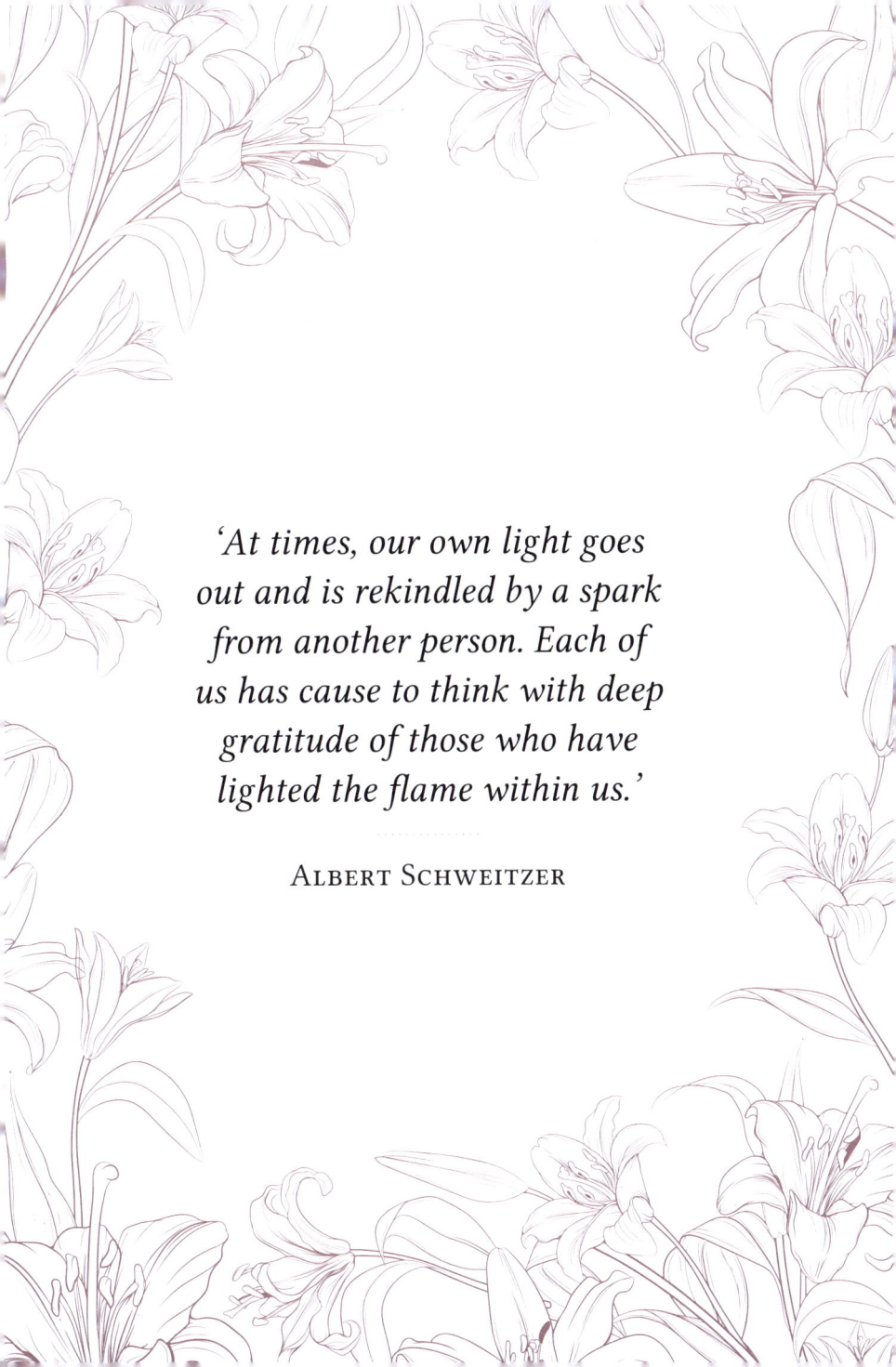

'At times, our own light goes out and is rekindled by a spark from another person. Each of us has cause to think with deep gratitude of those who have lighted the flame within us.'

ALBERT SCHWEITZER

LEVELLING

George Lee

Blessings. I have been given a lot. So many things I'm truly thankful for – our country, my freedoms, the family I was born into, the wonderful person I met on the second day in my first job, the life we have shared, the loving family we have reared, the magic and joy and renewal our grandchildren now bring.

Luck in career too. Economics. Journalism. Broadcasting. A short stint in the Dáil; and RTÉ, where I found my groove and have stayed put for the past 32 years.

I am grateful, of course, for that relative success, but some of it comes from things that I am strong in, and luck and decisions that made my life smoother.

The thing is, you see, it's when I am weakest, and not strong, that gratitude grips me the most.

Two years ago, a massive eruption of a lumbar disc severely compressed my spinal cord. I lost control of my legs, my bladder, my bowels, and more. It's called Cauda Equina Syndrome. For a short while, a lifetime of incontinence, confined to a wheelchair, seemed to stretch out before me.

But surgeons and doctors and nurses, all strangers to me, moved quickly to save me. Their skills and expertise, their concern

· GRATITUDE ·

and professionalism, which I got for free, are the only reason I am walking today, fully in control of my bodily functions.

So, I think I know what gratitude is.

Gratitude humbles. It levels. It reminds us that we can all be vulnerable and weak, that health and happiness, comfort and position, can disappear in a flash. It underscores how we need to care for each other, to be charitable to each other, and to forgive.

For me, gratitude is the reflection of something important at the core of our humanity.

George Lee is an Irish economist, journalist, television and radio presenter. He is the environment correspondent for RTÉ News.

'Old friends pass away, new friends appear. It is just like the days. An old day passes, a new day arrives. The important thing is to make it meaningful: a meaningful friend or a meaningful day.'

DALAI LAMA

· GRATITUDE ·

DOING THE RIGHT THING

Ger Deering

I'm grateful I wasn't born in Gaza. I grew up in a safe and secure environment with loving parents who had the opportunity, motivation, determination and ability to nurture and support my three siblings and me.

I'm grateful to have been blessed with two wonderful children who grew up in safety and security – free from tyranny and oppression. I'm grateful I didn't have to watch them starve to death or drag them limbless or lifeless from the rubble of a home cruelly demolished as the world stood idly by.

I'm grateful to those who helped me to think independently and recognise right from wrong, to recognise injustice, and those who inspired me to right wrongs where I can. I'm grateful to have had the opportunity to apply the values of fairness and justice in the various roles I've been so fortunate to hold, and the opportunity to make a positive difference in some people's lives.

Despite my own good fortune, I'm sad with the state of the world. Man's inhumanity to man is more evident than ever. I'm grateful for leaders who demand killings to stop and human rights to prevail – I despair of those who won't. I'm grateful for the millions of people at home and abroad who are calling and fighting for justice.

I'm grateful for the hope that Ireland will be on the right side of history in doing what we can to stop the slaughter and starvation of innocent men, women, children and babies in Palestine. I'm hopeful that we will also do the right thing for our vulnerable people and those seeking refuge here.

I have much to be grateful for, especially the solace and joy I get from nature, my garden, the colleagues I work with, the friends I've made, my family and those dear to me.

....

Ger Deering is Ombudsman, Information Commissioner, Commissioner for Environmental Information and Commissioner for Protected Disclosures. He is a member of the Electoral Commission, the Standards in Public Office Commission and the Commission for Public Service Appointments. He was previously the Financial Services and Pensions Ombudsman and Director of the National Employment Rights Authority.

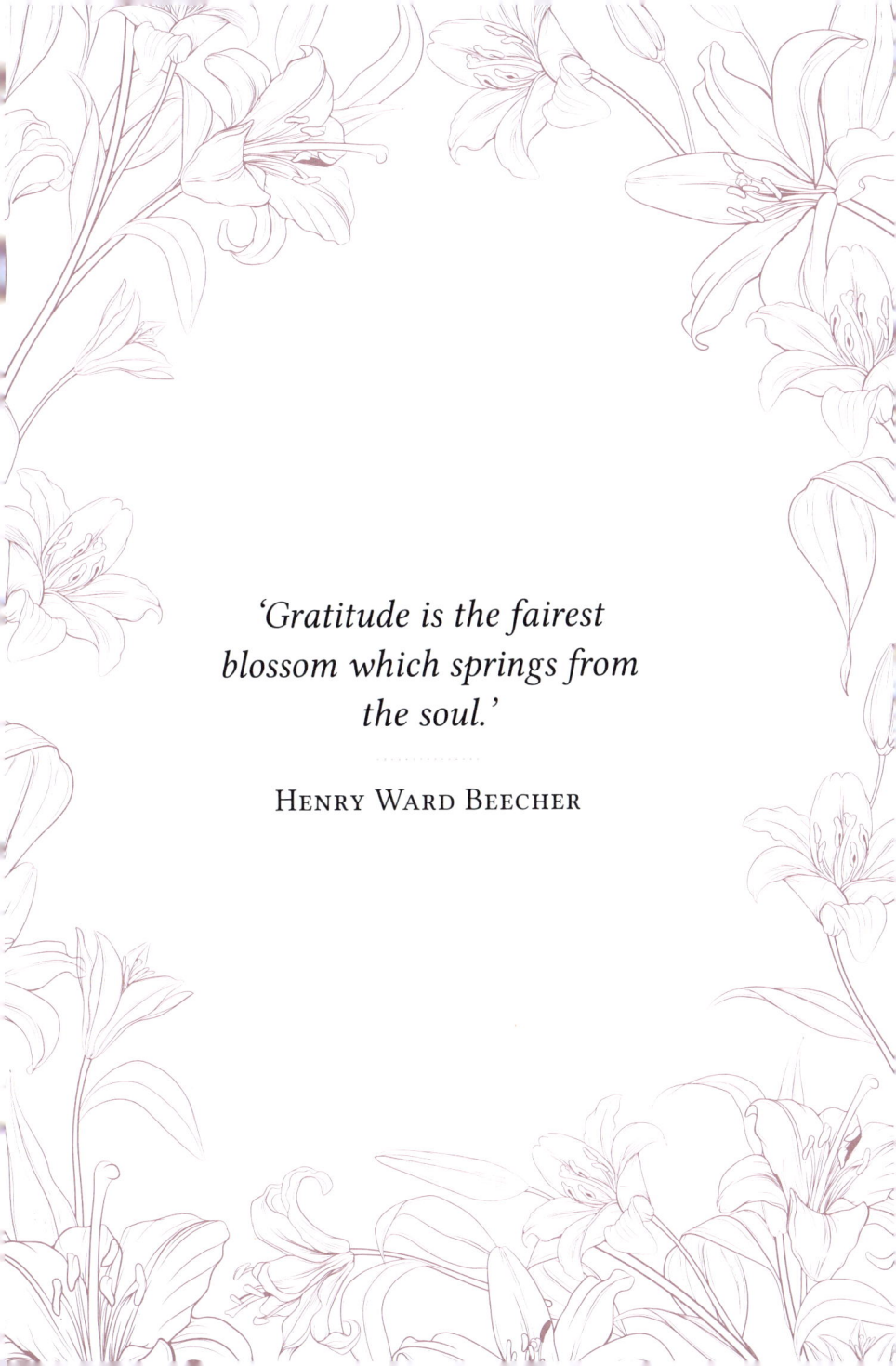

'Gratitude is the fairest
blossom which springs from
the soul.'

Henry Ward Beecher

… SR STAN …

GRATITUDE IS LOVE

Gráinne Seoige

Sometimes it can be difficult to connect to gratitude when you feel problems or stresses are mounting up. If that is what is occupying the mind, it can become a negative spiral, and it is then hard to see the positive.

I find that thinking about stuff that is close to me and fills my heart is what can help me pivot, like the welcome my dog has for me when I walk in the front door, photos of my family – especially my niece and nephews – remembering being in nature, whether in Connemara or near Cape Town; accessing that feeling of being very small indeed in the face of the magnificence of nature gives me perspective and reminds me that there is a lot to be grateful for.

Essentially what works for me to trigger gratitude – is love.

Gráinne Seoige is a broadcaster who has been on our screens since 1996. From the first days of TnaG, to the launch of TV3 and then Sky News Ireland, she has been at the forefront of television history. Gráinne continues to work across the channels in Ireland as Gaeilge agus i mBéarla, making programmes ranging from chat shows and documentaries on women's health, to dating shows with a very Irish twist.

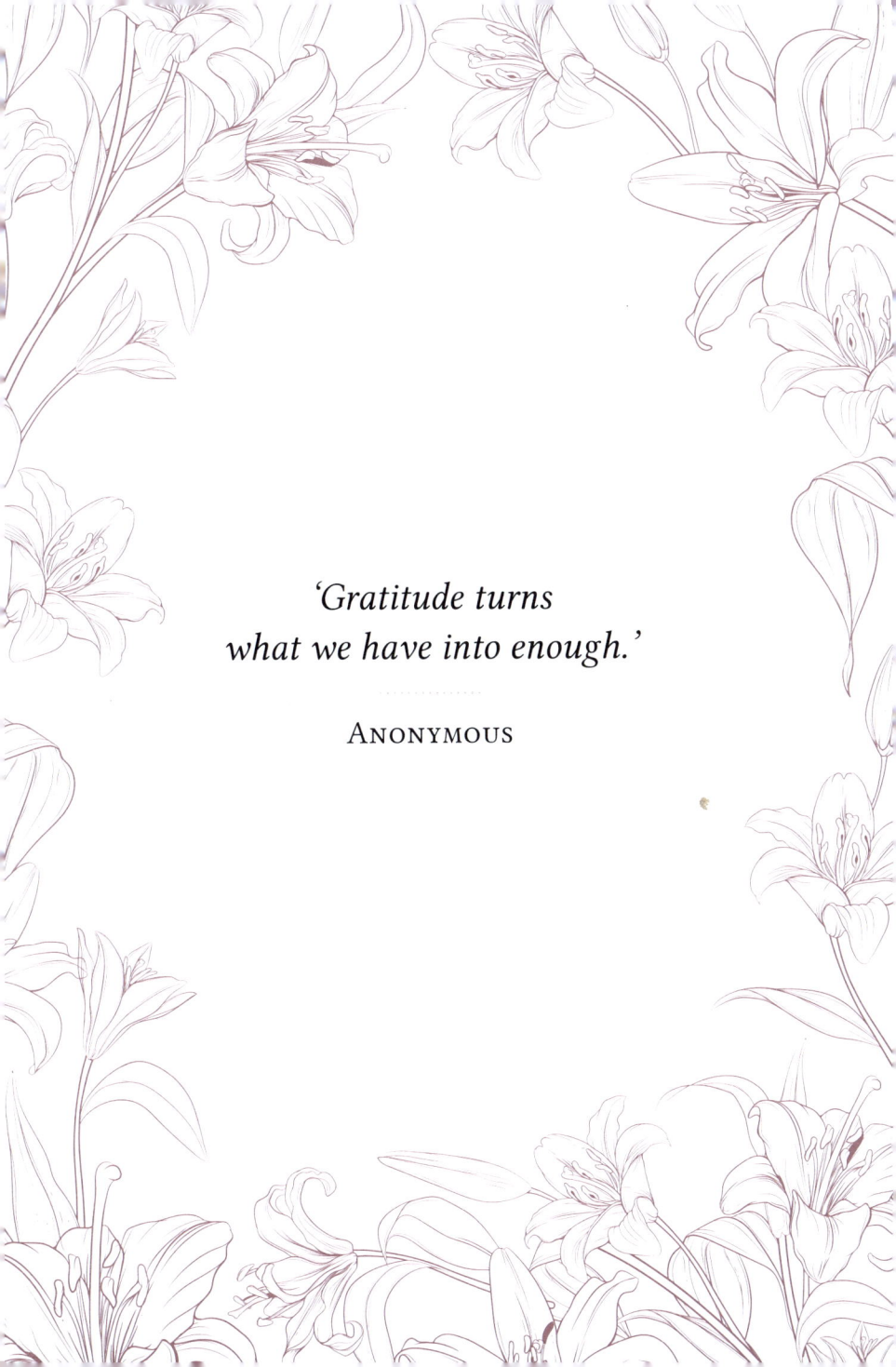

'Gratitude turns
what we have into enough.'

Anonymous

CENTRALITY OF GRATITUDE

Michael Rashid

(aka Haikal Mansor)

Growing up as a young Rohingya boy with constrained opportunities and the state-sanctioned grave human rights abuses in the pariah state of Burma, the centrality of gratitude that my mother instilled in me has shaped my way of life.

My mother, whose citizenship was stripped, and whose husband was forced into exile by the Burmese military junta, leaving her to take the roles of both father and mother, has often used *shukr* while raising us amidst a future of uncertainty.

For her, *shukr*, a Rohingya word derived from Arabic which means gratitude, is a form of worship and a pillar of life. Whether they are the manmade calamities or the tribulations of God, she never forgets to count countless blessings and expresses gratitude through her heart, tongue and acts.

In our darkest of days, she has been always the light that lightens up not only our worlds, but also our minds.

'The key to happiness and contentment lies in gratitude. Your father may not be here with us, but I go to bed with your love, care and warmth every night, and I wake up with resilience and hope seeing your faces every morning. What else can I ask for?' I vividly recall my mother's words of gratitude on one of the evenings as I was giving her a massage to her arms, shoulders and legs, which were covered with third-degree burns.

She is the two-way mirror through which I see the world and my world in hers, despite being separated by the man-engraved borders and cages across continents for 18 years.

In a world where the rhetoric of hate and intolerance, the inferno of chaos and violence, the shattering inequalities and the looming climate disasters attempt to dictate the future, I see gratitude as central to being content, caring for and appreciating what we have, and creating a sense of giving back to the communities for a better future.

································

Haikal Mansor (Hichael Rashid) is a member of the long-persecuted Rohingya community from Burma, where he was born and grew up. He arrived in Ireland in 2010 to pursue the dream of seeking knowledge and education. He lives in Carlow while investing in the development of the resettled Rohingya community in Ireland, particularly youth education.

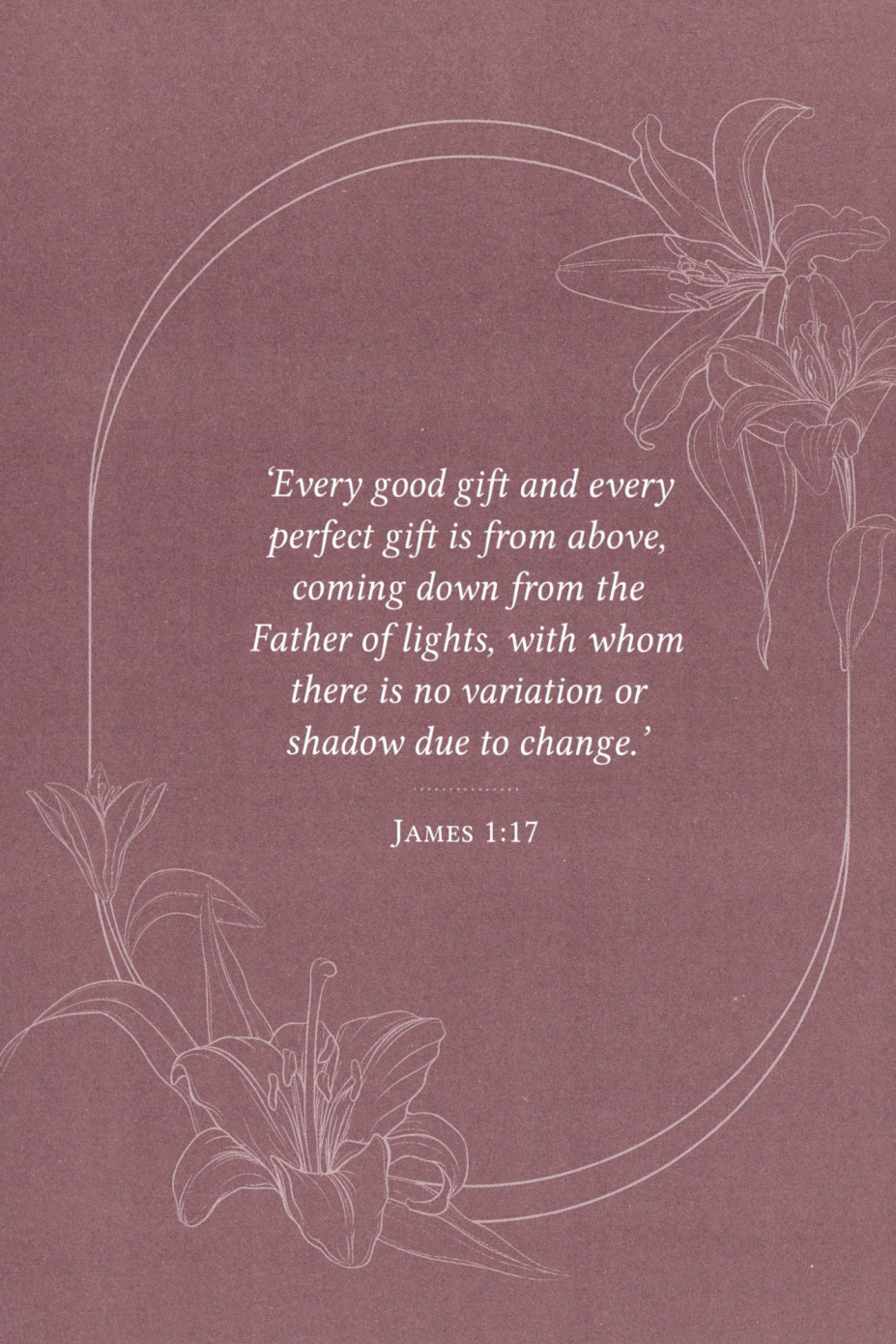

'Every good gift and every perfect gift is from above, coming down from the Father of lights, with whom there is no variation or shadow due to change.'

JAMES 1:17

BE LOVED

Harry Goddard

It was pitch-dark as we ascended the external staircase of a block of council flats. The spiral staircase was encased in a concrete cylinder that matched the height of the entire block, with short bridges extending to each floor. Other than the occasional light bleeding from a door or window, the scene was in complete darkness.

It was a cold winter night. We were on our way to visit the daughter of a lady whom we had just met. Heavily tattooed and tough, she had managed to become independent of her own previously violent relationship, and had already lost a son to drugs. She had described her daughter's addiction and the impact it had on her and her granddaughter. Her granddaughter was enrolling in beauty school to become a nail technician and, as a young adult, seemed to be uninterested in and unaffected by the habits that had impacted her own mother.

She talked about how addiction had wrecked the lives of her family whom she clearly loved. We were ascending the stairs to her daughter's flat to encourage her to participate in a residential rehab programme she was signed up for. Of course, she didn't want to go, leaving her own daughter behind and risking losing her flat.

Thinking of the experiences of the people I met that night, or the lesser challenges I have faced in my lifetime, I am grateful to be where I am today, surrounded by my family – parents, siblings, spouse and children. Love makes difficult circumstances tolerable and inspiring ones exceptional; it defines our experience of life. I am grateful to have learnt this lesson. Most especially, I am grateful to love and be loved.

• •

Harry Goddard is the CEO of Deloitte Ireland LLP.

'Gratitude is a powerful catalyst for happiness. It's the spark that lights a fire of joy in your soul.'

AMY COLLETTE

MAKING A DIFFERENCE

Heather Humphreys

First and foremost, on a personal level, my husband and I are blessed to have had two beautiful daughters, and for that I will always be grateful. Just three years ago, I was delighted to become a grandmother for the first time to a lovely little boy, who was joined just three months ago by a little sister. All these things may seem like the normal course of life, but I never take for granted the gift of new life, and the joy of becoming a mother and a grandmother for the first time, and the happiness it brings.

I have been most fortunate to have met many remarkable people during my life. I will always be grateful to two great female teachers in secondary school – one who instilled in me a love of politics, and another who was an independent thinker who encouraged me to speak up and not be afraid to give an opinion.

I am grateful for the women who inspired me, but particularly grateful to my mother who always made me feel there was no job a woman could not do.

When I worked in the credit union, I was grateful to be able to make a real difference in people's lives, and to help them overcome the many challenges that face us all.

· GRATITUDE ·

To the people of counties Monaghan and Cavan, I will be forever grateful to them for placing their trust in me, and for the opportunity they have given me on three occasions to represent them in Dáil Éireann. This has meant that I have had the honour and privilege of serving as a minister for almost ten years.

I am incredibly grateful for the opportunities I have had during my term as a minister, whether it be leading the 2016 commemorations, helping businesses prepare for Brexit, dealing with the Covid pandemic, the transformation of rural Ireland, or the many reforms I have spearheaded in social protection.

Finally, I am grateful for good health and great energy to carry out my duties, so that I can make a positive difference in people's lives.

Heather Humphreys is an Irish Fine Gael politician who has served in various cabinet positions since 2014, currently serving as Minister for Rural and Community Development and Minister for Social Protection since June 2020.

'Nothing is more honourable
than a grateful heart.'

LUCIUS ANNAEUS SENECA

· GRATITUDE ·

FINDING THE SPACE TO BE GRATEFUL IN AN IMPERFECT WORLD

Ian Hyland

When I think of gratitude, the unforgettable line from Seamus Heaney's 'The Cure at Troy' comes to mind. 'It was a fortunate wind that blew me here.' I think of this line often when the frustrations of personal or professional life visit my doorstep.

In a fast-moving world, driven by material metrics of success, it is too easy to lose perspective, as we all do, to forget those less fortunate, and lose sight of meaningful values.

I am one of these very people who can get caught in the whirlwind of keeping pace with one's self and peers, and often forget the simple mantra: 'There is no roof rack on a hearse.'

To counter this, I try, not always successfully, to use the skills developed over my personal and professional journey to give people the tools to help themselves, when it has been my good fortune to be in a position where I can offer help. There is no greater feeling of worth and meaning.

If you are Irish, you know only too well that intelligence and ability are evenly distributed, but opportunity and the breaks of life are not. Therefore, and having spent many years working with wonderful people, projects and causes across Haiti, Africa, the United States and Ireland, I have had the privilege of witnessing how giving can be so much more gratifying than receiving.

Sr Stanislaus Kennedy's luminous work on gratitude shines forth, guiding us towards a deeper understanding of thankfulness.

So maybe we should all take two minutes, close the laptop, drop the phone and think of the small gesture we can take today that can make a positive impact on others. Life can be simple if we choose it to be!

'The roots of all goodness lie in the soil of appreciation for goodness' – Dalai Lama.

Ian Hyland is president of Business & Finance, Ireland INC, and chairman and publisher at Quartet Book Publishing.

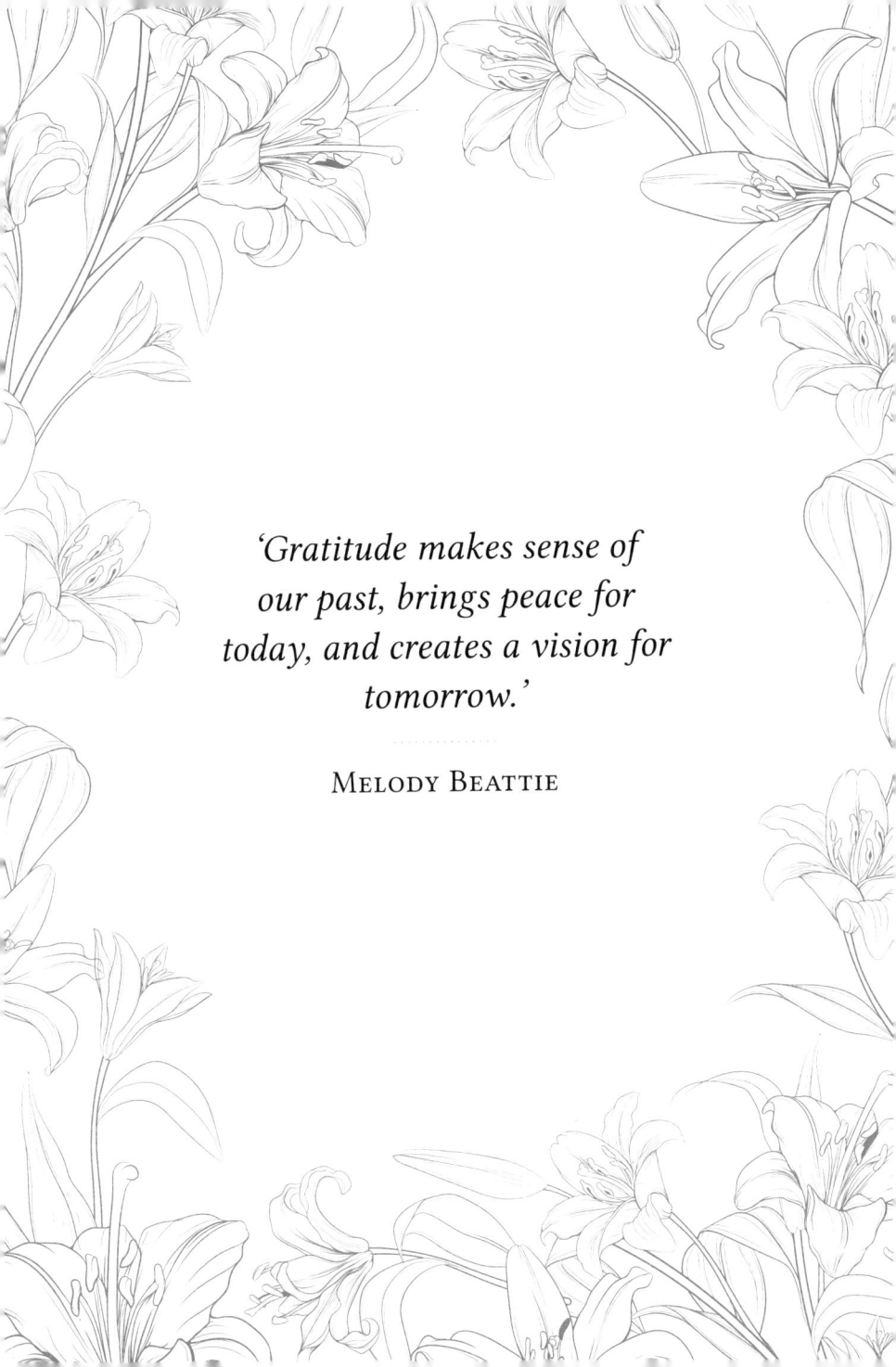

'Gratitude makes sense of our past, brings peace for today, and creates a vision for tomorrow.'

Melody Beattie

GRATITUDE IN MY DAILY LIFE

Jane Ohlmeyer

In January 2024, while out for a walk near my home on Cruit Island, County Donegal, I slipped and fractured my ankle in two places. For six weeks, I was grounded in a full cast and, for four of them, I was totally helpless because I was unable to bear any weight on my left leg.

Since I live alone, it was an intense time, especially given what was going on in the world, but also a period for reflection, an unplanned break from my hectic work and travel schedule. On the foot of this (and do forgive the pun), I am profoundly grateful for so many things.

- For the neighbours who rescued me from a remote and grassy laneway, shopped for me, and minded me; a thermos of boiling water, brought by a neighbour after Storm Isha knocked out the electricity, made a most memorable cup of tea.
- For the local postman, who regularly checked in on me, and the taxi man, who every fortnight drove me to Letterkenny Hospital and sat with me as my foot was X-rayed, examined, and replastered by professional healthcare workers.

- For the technology that allowed me to work online with my amazing colleagues.
- For the friends and family who enveloped me in love as they sent me treats, called, cooked and kept my spirits high.
- For the magnificent and ever-changing views of Mount Errigal, the wildness of the waves, the howling winds, the driving rain, and the gentle winter sunshine. The painkillers took care of my ankle, and nature was a tonic for my soul.

In short, those six weeks reminded me of what really matters: a caring community, the love of family and friends, and, simply, going for a walk on a winter's day. For all of this, I am so desperately grateful.

Professor Jane Ohlmeyer, MRIA, FBA, FTCD, FRHistS, is Erasmus Smith's Professor of Modern History (1762) at Trinity College Dublin. She is the author of many books and articles, including Making Ireland: Ireland, Imperialism and the Early Modern World *(Oxford, 2023). In 2023, she was awarded the Royal Irish Academy Gold Medal in the Humanities.*

'The Lord bless you and keep you; the Lord make his face to shine upon you and be gracious to you; the Lord lift up his countenance upon you and give you peace.'

Numbers 6:24–26

· GRATITUDE ·

CATCHING APPLES

JD Buckley

I feel extremely grateful to have lived in a happy house growing up. My mum and dad are both amazing people who taught me so much. They've both got a great work ethic, and I'm lucky that some of that rubbed off on me.

I'm also hugely grateful to my wife, Fleur, for acquiescing to my overtures many years ago. Without Fleur, I would be nowhere. She is possibly the only person who could have tolerated me for all these years. She keeps me on my toes and down to earth. We are lucky to be able to have fun together every day, but also to have three amazing boys, each of whom brings us enormous happiness.

And finally, I'm so grateful for the job that I get to do every day. I have a job which I love, and I'm lucky that I get to work with the people I work with each day (or at least almost every day!). Not many people can say that. And despite what people might think from the outside looking in, a lot of success in business is being in the right place at the right time. If you give yourself enough opportunities, the apple will fall.

JD Buckley is CEO of Sky Ireland and has led the Irish business since 2012. JD is responsible for Sky's consumer and media divisions, driving the growth of the overall business and leading a team of 1,000 employees in Ireland.

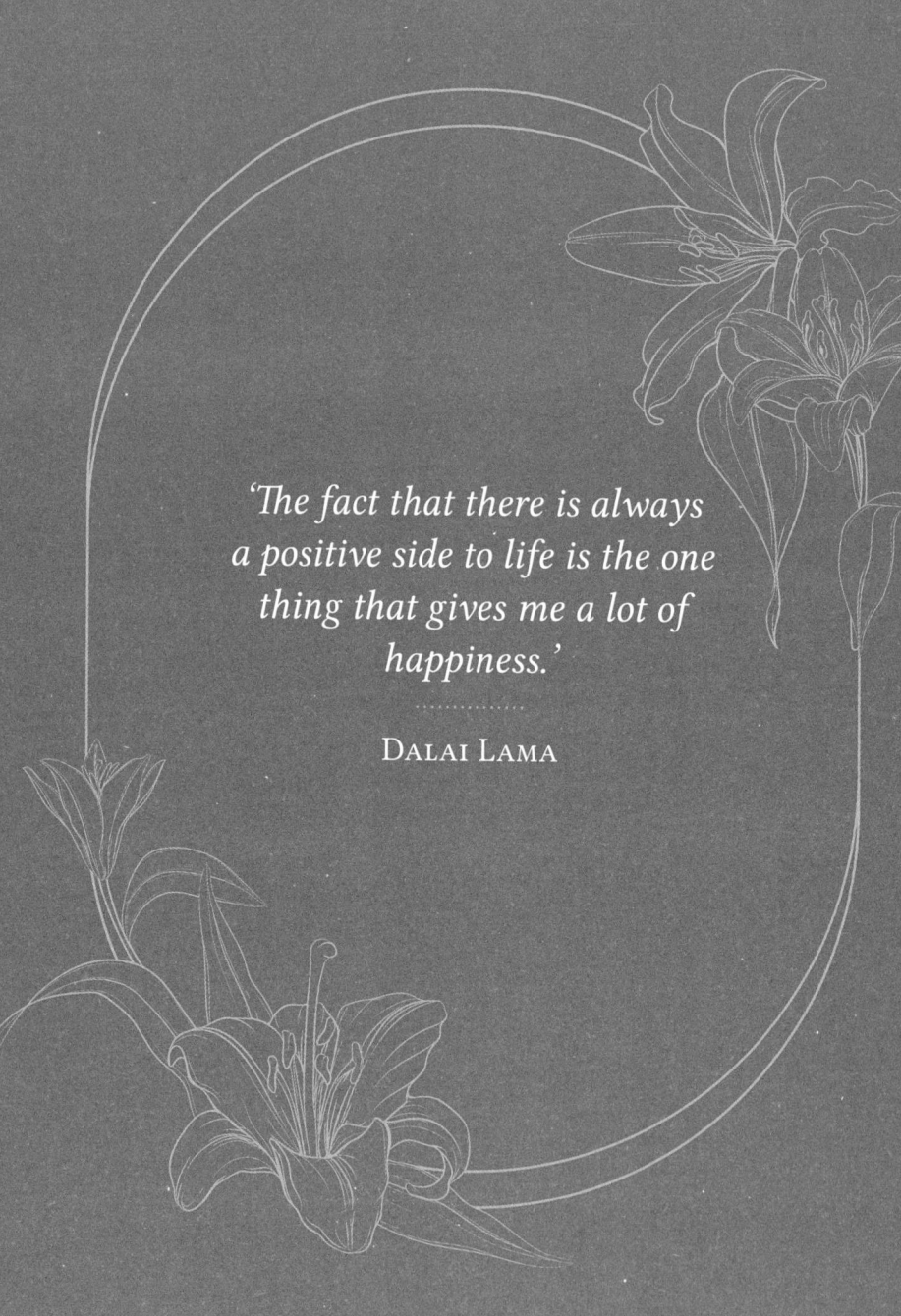

'The fact that there is always a positive side to life is the one thing that gives me a lot of happiness.'

DALAI LAMA

· GRATITUDE ·

WHO DO I THANK

John Clarke

I have been thinking about the concept of gratitude, and how frequently (or otherwise) we use it.

I think its meaning gets blurred when you really don't know who to thank. In times past, we could always thank our particular deity for the benefits and kindness bestowed upon us. That gratitude now seems blurred, and it is difficult to find a reference point that makes any sense.

Currently, I have countless defects and illnesses due to old age. Who do I thank?

Who do I feel grateful to? The doctors who prescribe medications, the pharmacist, and all that long list of people who keep me alive. I am very grateful that they do, but to whom do I show my gratitude? I am very much aware of endless people, friends, relatives etc., who contribute to my well-being, and I certainly revere them with a deep sense of gratitude.

All my life, I have always looked on the bright side, despite day-to-day disasters, and I have found something positive to be grateful for. By and large, it makes *me* feel better if I can remember the positives of my life rather than the negatives; from the small child in Africa who was overjoyed with a slice of bread, I shared his joy and his gratitude that together we could make him less hungry for today and, in doing so, added to my share of being, but this concept of gratitude, however fleeting, adds to *my* positivity.

If I can give an example – when my wife died, I was in a black hole of despair; but later, I thought, she had a perfect death which most people would wish for. She died in her sleep without pain and without knowing it. I felt deep gratitude that she did not have to suffer or go through the trauma of a lingering and painful death. My heart filled with gratitude for this blessing. Who do I thank?

To my wife's chagrin, I have always loved the sound of the Angelus, and the sound of the muezzin calling the adhān prayer. These, by and large, occur around the same time. My wife could not get her head around the idea that I loved to pause and wonder – who or what I am. These sounds make me stop and think and feel grateful for all the good things that have happened in my life.

* * *

John Clarke has recently written about life and love with his late wife Marian Finucane. He received the Philanthropist of the Year Award (International) in 2009 from the Community Foundation of Ireland for the work himself and Marian did in South Africa, which spanned 15 years from 2003. He lives in Co. Kildare and is keeping himself busy with the construction of a Zen garden at his home. He estimates the first stage of this project will take 40 years to complete. He is currently 88 and of sound mind.

'Thankfulness is the beginning of gratitude. Gratitude is the completion of thankfulness. Thankfulness may consist merely of words. Gratitude is shown in acts.'

Henri Frederic Amiel

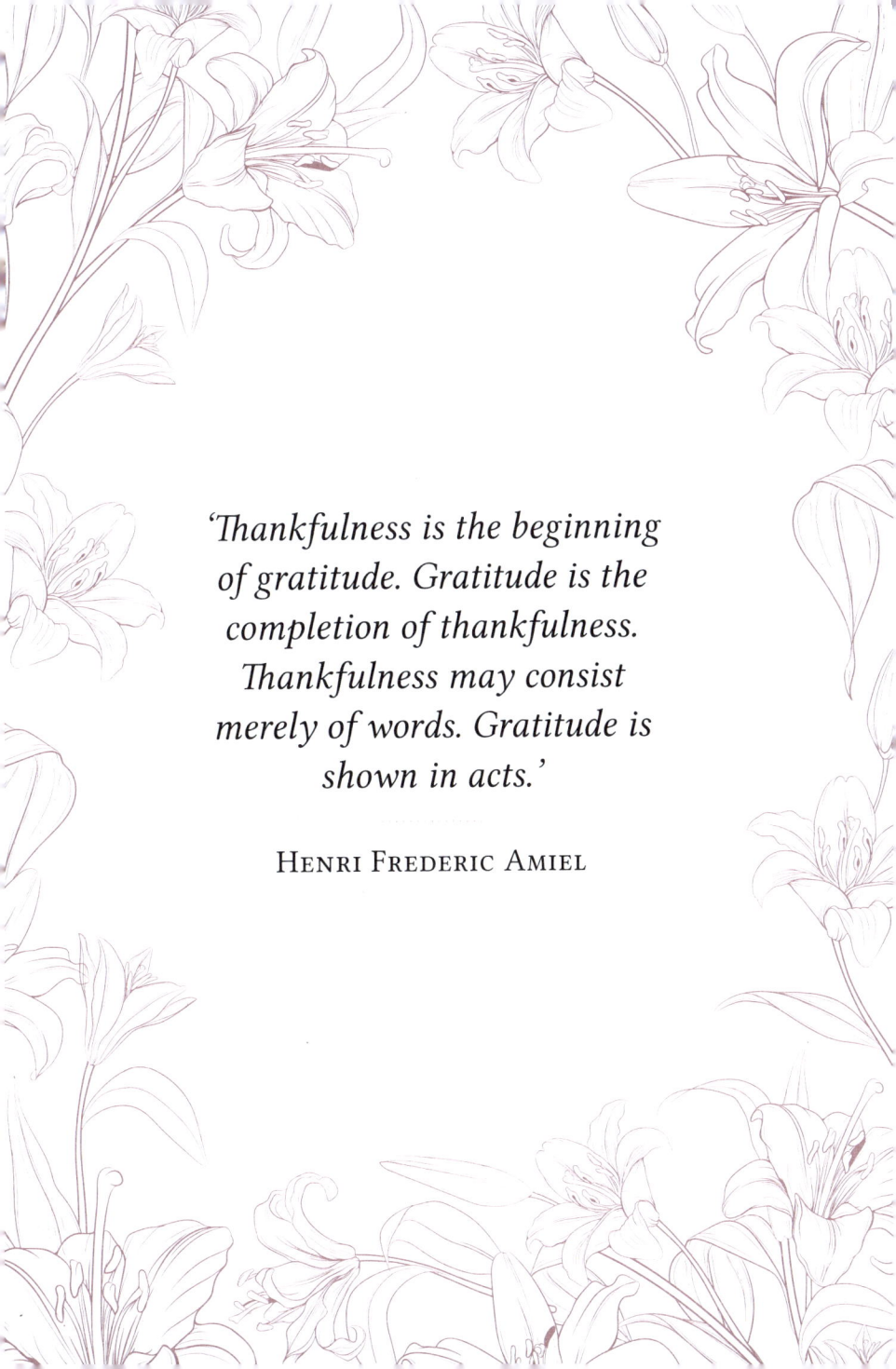

MY GRATEFUL PLACE

John Cunningham

As I get older, I try to spend as much time in my 'grateful place' as I can. Being in this place makes me feel safe, reassured and happy. I am grateful that I have developed this awareness with time. It is easy to talk about how important it is to surround yourself with good and positive people, but I have found that I am most grateful when I am aware of and connected to nature – the sky, the sun, trees, flowers, the wind. This is a place that grounds me and allows me to leave the toxic and draining elements of daily life behind.

Sometimes it is hard to find the grateful place, and you have to make an effort to 'find it'. That can require finding a quiet space in the day and just hand yourself over to the stillness (not always easy, but so worthwhile!).

· GRATITUDE ·

I have also found that the more grateful you are, the easier it is to help others – to leverage that 'power of one' we all have. I am a better person when I live a grateful life.

I am grateful for the gift of love – don't be afraid to say it, and don't ever assume that people know you love them. Tell them as often as possible – it doesn't diminish its impact.

In stating the obvious, I will often end a text or a conversation with someone saying 'we all have so much to be grateful for.' We reside in the top 1% of people on the planet. From the point of view of privilege and opportunity, we have little to complain about.

John Cunningham is the Relationship Director for Morgan McKinley, Dublin.

'Oh give thanks to the Lord, for he is good, for his steadfast love endures forever!'

Psalm 107:1

· GRATITUDE ·

I'M GRATEFUL FOR...

Justine McCarthy

I'm grateful for a night's sleep.
To open my eyes in the morning and be alive.
To hear birds chattering and schoolchildren hastening beneath my window.
To measure the stretch in the spring evenings.
To spy the daffodils poking to life.
To feel the Atlantic waves in Barley Cove that swallow me.
To smell fried garlic.
To lick a '99' on a hot day.
To be healthy.
To hear my native townspeople recall my parents with affection.
To be with my sisters, who make me laugh and allow me to cry.
To have memories of my husband that keep him near.
To see my son's capacity to show love.
To know I am loved.
To be called 'friend' by my friends.
To feel hopeful when Leonard Cohen sings 'there is a crack in everything – that's how the light gets in.'
To be asked my opinion.
To have witnessed the indomitability of the human spirit throughout my career.

To be paid for work that is a privilege.

For the lump in my throat when the Pearl Fishers sing their duet.

For the kindness of strangers.

For the stories of our lives.

For happy coincidences.

For peace in Ireland.

For the intimacy of Ireland.

For the taxi driver who refused my money when my child had an accident in the schoolyard.

For the woman who called to me across a Dublin Bus, 'Are you William McCarthy's daughter?' – six decades after he died.

For good people who enter political life despite its thanklessness.

For the right to vote.

For volunteers and nurses and doctors and rescuers.

For the film-makers and painters, the playwrights and poets who pour over us.

For getting into a warm bed at night.

For the novel under the lamplight that lures me into other lives.

For being able to drift off at day's end with a roof above my head.

Justine McCarthy is a columnist with the Irish Times *and an author. She has won more than a dozen awards for her journalism, including the Broadsheet Columnist of the Year three times.*

'Happiness cannot be travelled to, owned, earned, worn or consumed. Happiness is the spiritual experience of living every minute with love, grace, and gratitude.'

Denis Waitley

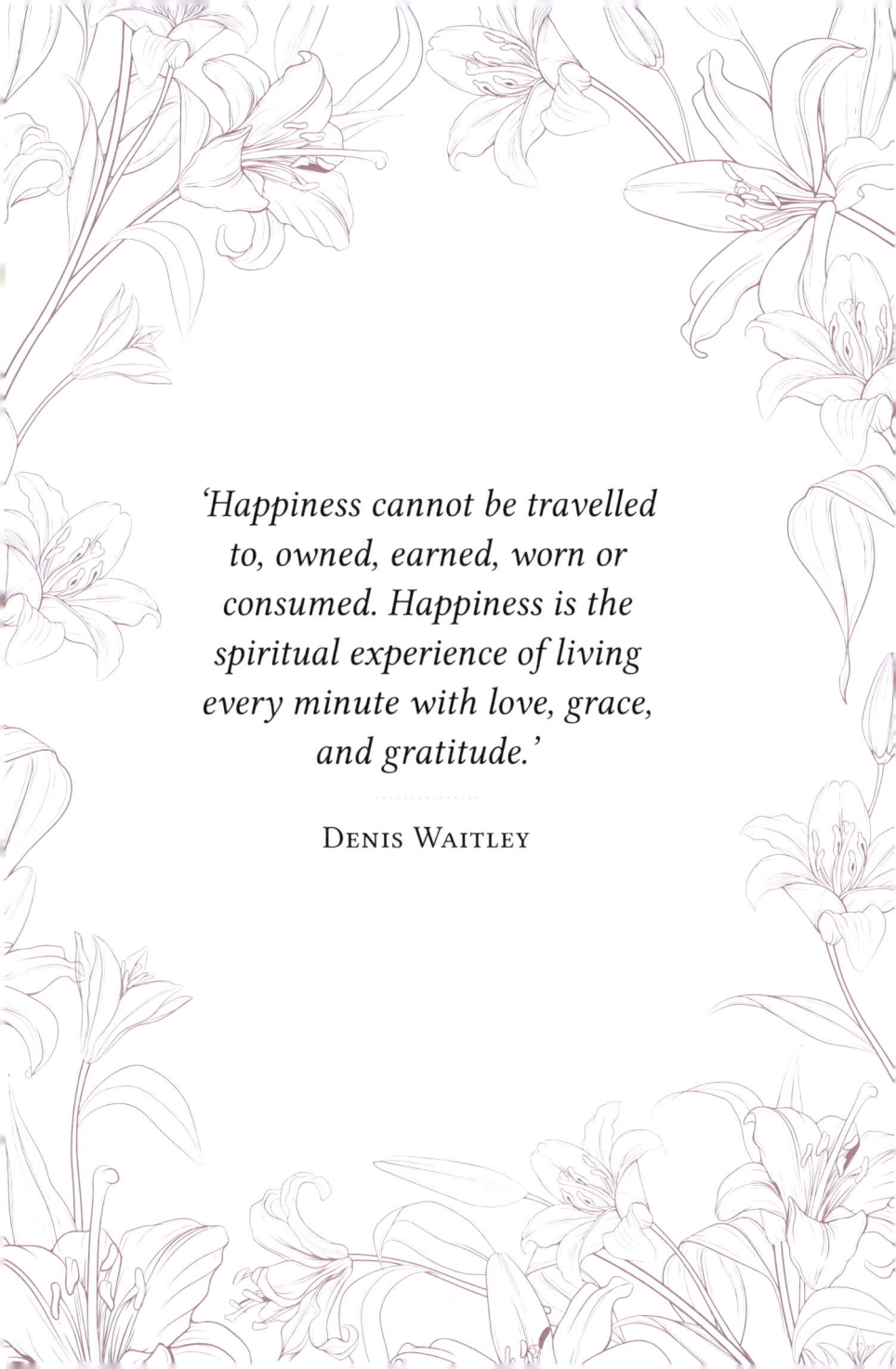

· SR STAN ·

LOOK FOR THE HELPERS

Kathy Sheridan

My family has had a torrid decade of illness. I had no sooner recovered from cancer than my husband, Pat, father to our two daughters, was diagnosed with a terminal brain tumour. Pat was greatly loved. He was witty, funny, highly entertaining, irreverent yet deeply kind.

Part of his appeal was the touch of Wilkins Micawber he had about him – Micawber being the optimistic character in Dickens's *David Copperfield* who, no matter what the crisis, fondly believed that 'something will turn up'. This had its downside when it came to planning and organising family life. As a woman who likes a plan, I freely admit to reacting poorly at times when no such plan was in evidence from the man of the house.

Yet this was precisely the trait which enabled him to endure his illness and reconcile us to his death. There was no self-pity from him. Those 21 months were borne with humour and patience, but above all with unshakeable gratitude for the extended family, the wonderful friends, the medics and the carers who treated him normally, took him on jaunts and shared our lives; and it was infectious.

Observing him, my lifelong loathing of 'inspirational quotes' was briefly abandoned in favour of this from Fred Rogers, an American famous for *Mister Rogers' Neighborhood*, an educational television programme for pre-schoolers: 'When I was a boy and I would see scary things in the news, my mother would say to me, "Look for the helpers. You will always find people who are helping."'

Pat saw that with startling clarity, so we did too. From the extraordinary nurse, Carol Browne, in the Mater's A&E department who sat with us when the catastrophic news was being delivered, to the Beaumont oncologist who literally ran room to room; from the Friends of St Luke's, who left inspirational poetry on the café tables, to the volunteers of Our Lady's Hospice, there were always the helpers.

Afterwards, when the busy world was hushed and we were left with the void, our daughters and I were reflecting on it all as we often did, when one of them said: 'Isn't it great that we're not angry ... that we have nothing to be angry about?'

And odd as it seems, it was true. A scary thing happened, and we looked for the helpers and they were there. We know too well that others on that path are not so lucky. Micawber was right. Something did turn up after all. And we are grateful beyond measure.

Kathy Sheridan is a columnist with the Irish Times *and co-host of The Women's Podcast.*

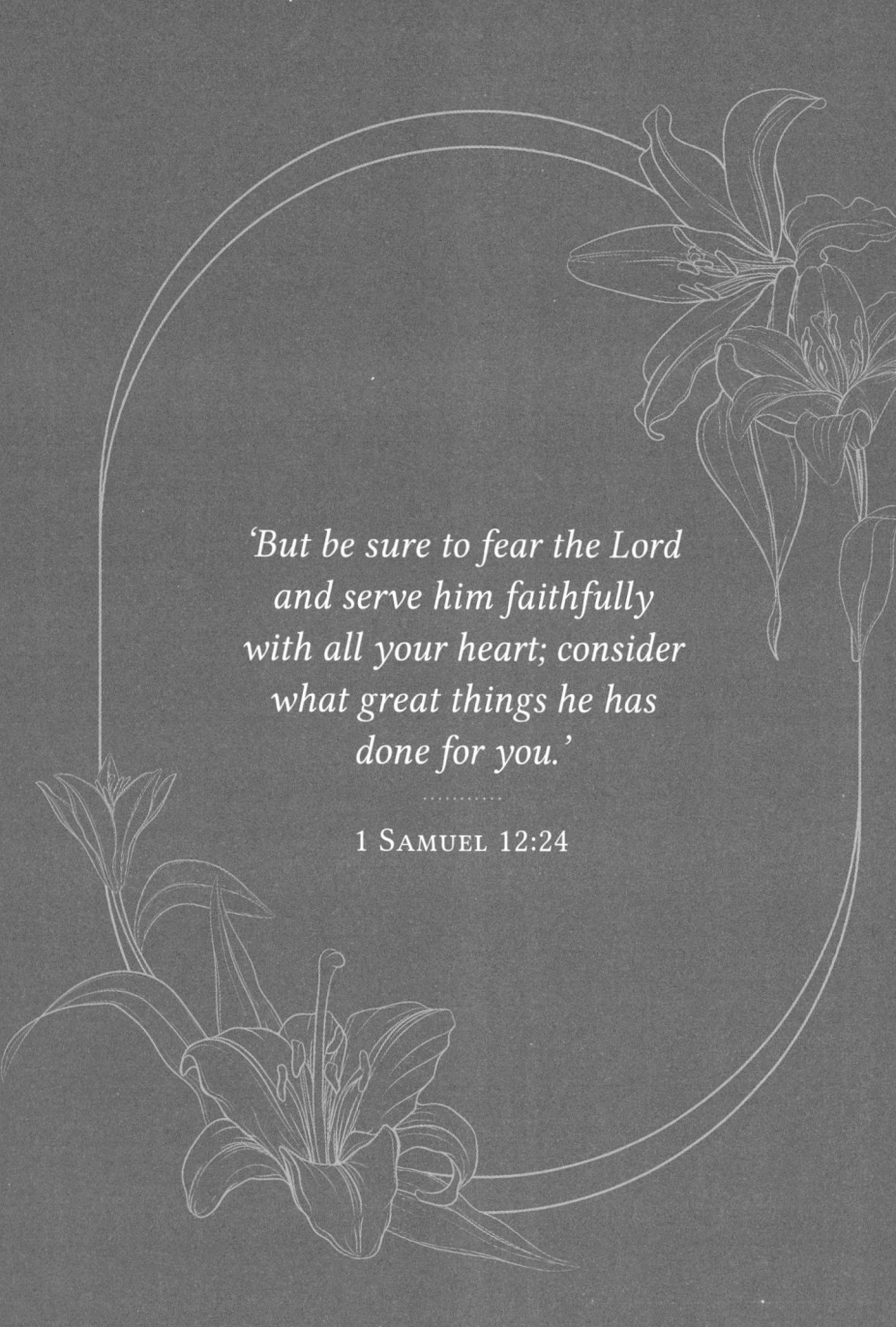

'But be sure to fear the Lord and serve him faithfully with all your heart; consider what great things he has done for you.'

1 Samuel 12:24

· GRATITUDE ·

SHINING A LIGHT

Kevin Bakhurst

The world this year seems more beset than ever by crisis, with war in Ukraine, horrendous civilian loss of life in Gaza and Israel, and the obvious effects of climate change. Against this background, the daily joys of life can sometimes feel overshadowed and small. But it is these seemingly small things that still provide a source of meaning and happiness for me and for many others.

The love and support of family and friends fills every day with light, and the addition of two beautiful grandchildren in the last couple of years has added to that personal joy – their first smiles, their excitement at discovering the world, their unquestioning love, and seeing my own children take on the responsibility and happiness of parenthood. In both cases, there is an extra joy in seeing the love of family dogs – and their gentleness applied to the new arrivals.

In Ireland, in the UK and on my travels, like so many, I find true happiness in the surroundings of nature – sea and mountains, rivers and trees. Such beauty is even more joyful when shared with loved ones (both human and canine). Then sometimes I will find it enhanced by manmade beauty – the ancient religious buildings at Glendalough, a small medieval church near my family home in Hertfordshire, the loving restoration of Notre Dame cathedral in Paris. Although not religious, those expressions of centuries-old hope and belief resonate deeply with me. I feel they are an ancient testament to a fundamental belief in kindness and tolerance, and I am grateful daily for the overall advances in tolerance and understanding that we see in today's society.

The huge advances in the acceptance of different types of family, the rights of women in society, the embracing and support of people of different sexuality or racial backgrounds – I have seen a remarkable sea-change even in my lifetime, and I salute the younger generation for leading the way.

In the face of so many global challenges, there remains so much to be grateful for that brings true meaning and joy to life – love, the beauty of our surroundings and tolerance of one another. Much worth fighting for and enjoying.

Kevin Bakhurst has been the Director General of RTÉ since July 2023. He previously worked at BBC News for many years and at the UK broadcast regulator Ofcom. He was born and brought up in North London. He is married to Barbara, has three grown-up children and two grandchildren.

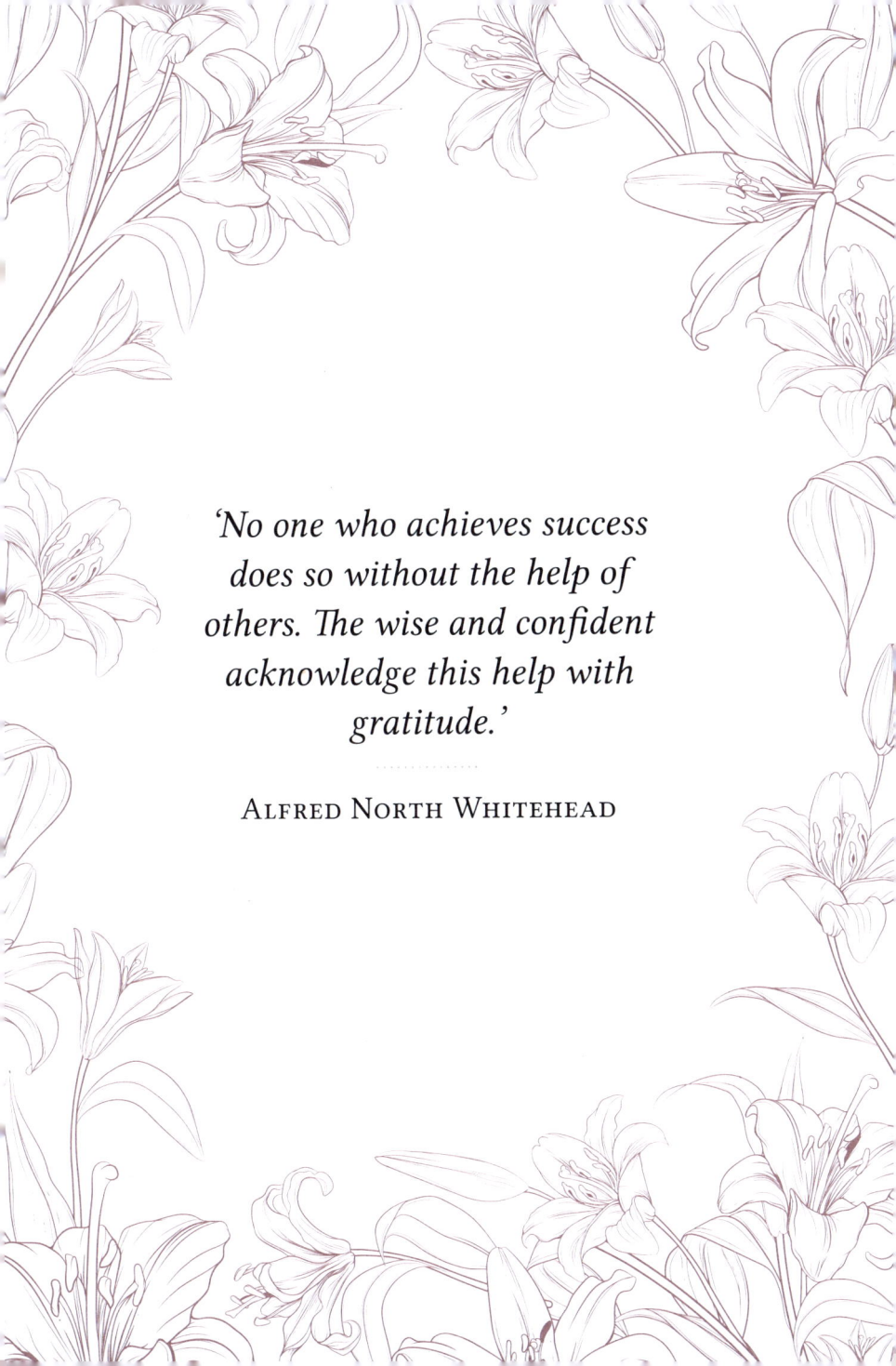

'No one who achieves success does so without the help of others. The wise and confident acknowledge this help with gratitude.'

ALFRED NORTH WHITEHEAD

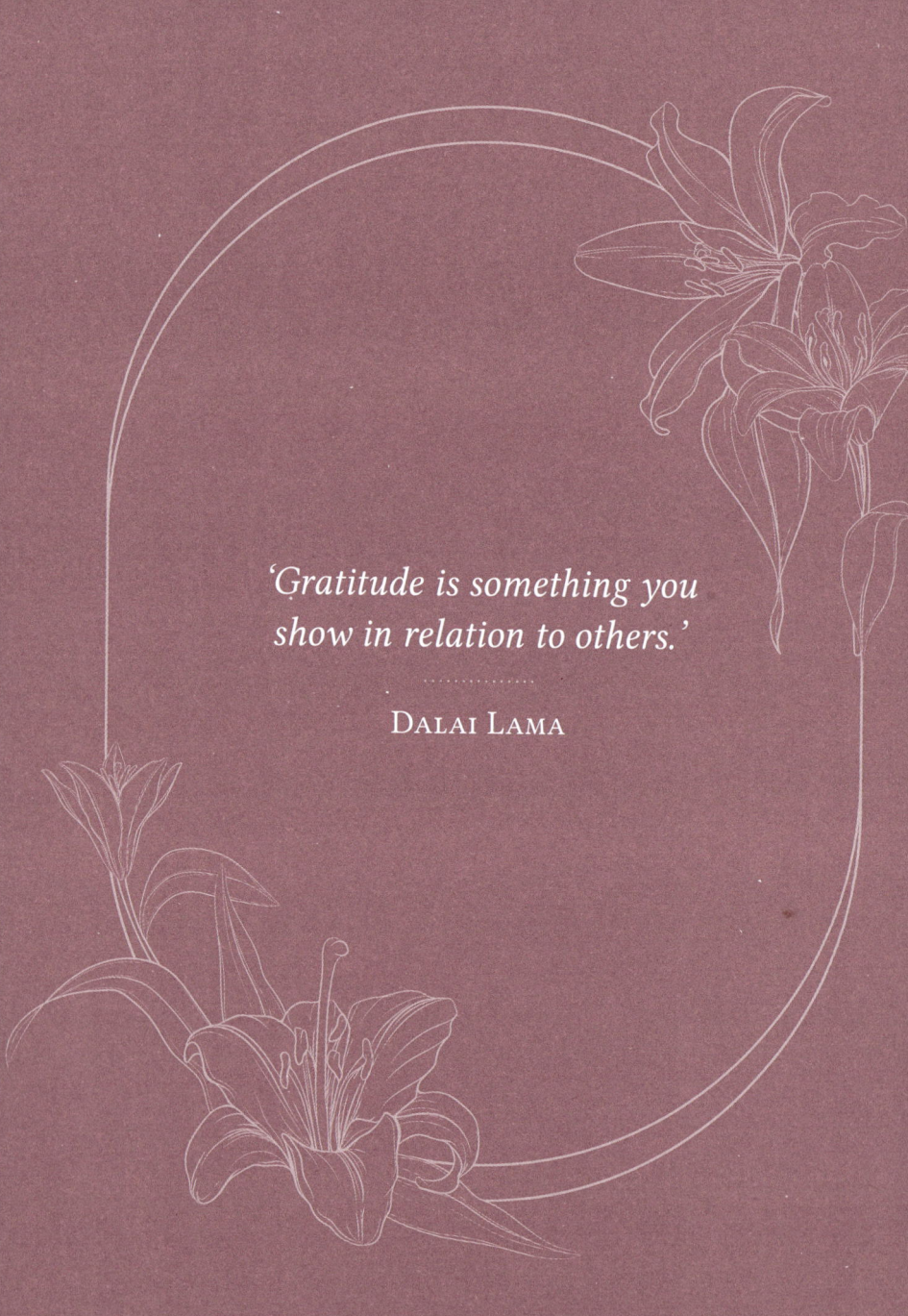

'Gratitude is something you show in relation to others.'

DALAI LAMA

· GRATITUDE ·

THE TIDE OF LOVE

Leo Varadkar

'When we focus on our gratitude, the tide of disappointment goes out and the tide of love rushes in' – Kristin Armstrong.

In the modern world, we are driven to want more, buy more, desire more. It is far too easy to forget to be grateful for all that we have and all that we have been given.

I am grateful to my parents for giving me a safe and stable home, for investing in my education and well-being.

I am grateful to my friends for being with me during good times and bad, for being on my side even when I didn't deserve it.

I am grateful to have been born and raised in Ireland, an imperfect country, but surely one of the best in a world of more than 200 nations.

I have travelled the world and seen its darkest places.

I know that for most people in the world, Ireland is paradise. What we regard as rights, they regard as luxuries.

We should be grateful for Ireland, love it, protect it and share it.

Leo Varadkar is an Irish Fine Gael politician who served as Taoiseach from 2017 to 2020, and from 2022 to 2024, as Tánaiste from 2020 to 2022, and as leader of Fine Gael from 2017 to 2024.

BIRDSONG

Linda Cullen

I am lucky to have a garden that is full of birds, so each morning at dawn I wake to birdsong. I sometimes snooze afterwards, but it's the most joyful sound, and steadies and grounds me for the day ahead.

My wife or I wake our children. They're teenagers now, so they stir when we open their blinds. I love to look at them as they waken, though I can't make it obvious; they are teens after all!

I drive them to school each day, and we listen to Spin on the radio, and more often than not we hear some young person losing the music quiz (no one ever wins it), and it tends to be the first belly laugh of the day, as we shout the answers at the radio; though we generally don't get it right either!

I feel gratitude for one positive that came out of the pandemic – hybrid working. I love my desk at home and the peace it affords me, and I love the buzz of the office when I am there.

I am grateful for my new tennis friends (another pandemic positive) who help keep me fit and laughing, my old friends who know me inside and out, and my colleagues – hard-working, fun, creative people.

· GRATITUDE ·

Mostly though, I am grateful for my family – my wife, my children, my brothers, my aunt and uncle, nieces, nephew, cousins. My mother is no longer here, but is truly present in so many ways, like my brother who died at 21. Although they are dead, they are alive, in me, in all who loved them. Daily.

As my little family winds down every evening, I sometimes still get a teenager laying her head on my lap to watch some TV before going to bed. I know this won't last forever, so I am grateful for every time it happens.

Linda Cullen is the CEO of COCO Content, one of Ireland's leading production companies.

'In ordinary life, we hardly realise that we receive a great deal more than we give, and that it is only with gratitude that life becomes rich.'

DIETRICH BONHOEFFER

· GRATITUDE ·

WHAT I AM GRATEFUL FOR...

Lisa-Nicole Dunne

As I grew up, I realised how many people do not have the privilege of coming from a loving, hard-working, decent family. I am so grateful for that: learning humility from my dad and siblings, confidence from how my mother raised us, and the support and friendship my family offer every single day.

I visited Johannesburg with UNICEF in 2009, and will never forget stepping over toddlers on stairs in a church where hundreds of unattached minors were living, having fled from Zimbabwe. It made me see how lucky I was to be born in Ireland, offered comfort and security for the most part through my geography.

I feel blessed with a strong mind that can change and likes uncertainty. I don't take this for granted. I am grateful for a positive disposition. Other things I am thankful for is the support of nurses, therapists and counsellors at Pieta for supporting the health and well-being of my family, and for nonprofits who are like the glue around society. Communities survive because of these; we often don't even realise they are there.

For the hope and progress that medical research offers.

I love to learn new things, from stoicism to AI, and I'm grateful for words, language and a changing world that is becoming more open and inclusive in many walks of life, although we have a long way to go.

The hugs, love and belief that come from my children and husband, their unbelievable love and the wonder they bring to every day. I am so proud and eternally grateful to have been blessed with Daniel, Sadie and Sophie.

For rainbows, butterflies and robins.

For music and the joy it brings.

For belly laughs with good friends and great colleagues.

For escapism through a good book or series.

And when all else fails, to still the mind, I am grateful for painting by numbers.

• •

Lisa-Nicole Dunne is CEO of Mantra Strategy, a strategic purpose and impact consultancy that helps organisations, brands and leaders to transform their impact and footprint in the world. She has led organisations through change and growth, and is strategic advisor to leaders at AsIAm, St Vincent de Paul, Pieta, Grow Mental Health and Coolmine Therapeutic Community.

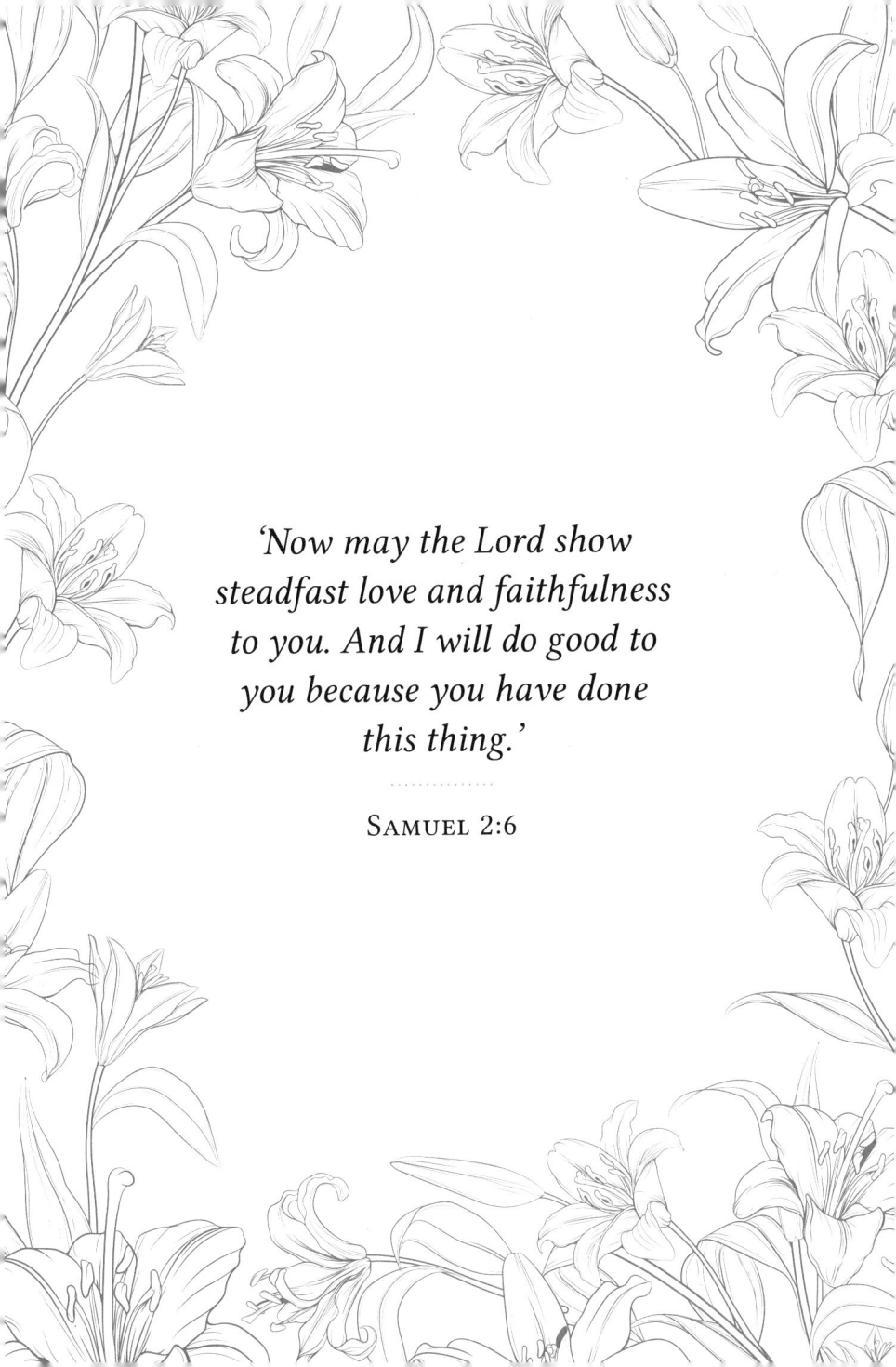

'Now may the Lord show
steadfast love and faithfulness
to you. And I will do good to
you because you have done
this thing.'

Samuel 2:6

THE MAKING OF ME

Liz O'Donnell

There is much for which I am grateful. I have had a good life, untouched so far by serious illness or disaster. I was privileged to have a meaningful career as a TD and government minister. I am grateful that Ireland is politically stable, and finally enjoying a precious peace. I have loved and been loved, and have two fine adult children and a loving partner. More than anything else, I am grateful that I was raised by loving parents, John and Carmel.

Carmel was one of six children born in the 1920s in the north inner city of Dublin. As a toddler, she contracted the polio virus, resulting in years of painful surgery to lengthen her lame leg and foot. Far from diminishing the child's spirit, these setbacks emboldened her personality, and she went on to play senior club camogie in her teens and twenties. It was through Gaelic games that she met my father, John, a talented hurler who played on the Dublin team in the 1940s, as well as being an Irish champion sprinter. So, it was sport, not politics, which cemented my family's connectedness with community and public service.

A great storyteller, Mum would regale us with hilarious Joycean-like tales of daily life in Dublin. Always happy, she radiated that positive disposition to us, her children. My father's secure job with the Guinness brewery meant we had more than most people in our street. We lived in the warm embrace of my maternal grandmother, my aunts and cousins. Unusual for the time, my father was a very hands-on dad, bringing us all over the country to athletics events, or to the beach at Dollymount on summer days.

Later, as a young woman TD, juggling a political career with two small children, my parents' support was essential, at times moving into my house during elections. My biggest fans, they stayed up late every night to watch *Oireachtas Report* on TV, just in case I might appear!

After politics, I cherished the time I had with them in their final years. I am forever grateful for the blessing of a happy childhood and wonderful parents. To quote Thomas Edison, they were 'the making of me'.

Liz O'Donnell was born in Dublin, and educated in Limerick and at Trinity College Law School. She was a Progressive Democrats TD for Dublin South for fifteen years, and served as Minister of State in the Department of Foreign Affairs, representing the Government at the multi-party talks leading to the Good Friday Agreement in 1998. She is currently chair of the Road Safety Authority.

'Gratitude is not only the greatest of virtues but the parent of all others.'

MARCUS TULLIUS CICERO

· GRATITUDE ·

THE STRENGTH OF CONNECTION

Louise Phelan

In the face of adversity, I find solace in the gratitude I carry within me. I am grateful for the journey I have embarked upon, and for all that I have accomplished thus far. Each step forward, each milestone achieved, fills my heart with a deep sense of appreciation, but I couldn't do it alone.

Firstly, I am immensely grateful for my parents and the love they showed. Their unwavering support and sacrifices have shaped me into the person I am today. Their belief in the power of education has instilled in me a thirst for knowledge and a drive for success.

I am also grateful for the incredible bond I share with my seventeen siblings. Together, we have experienced both triumphs and tribulations, but it is through these shared experiences that our connection grows stronger. In times of trouble, their presence serves as a reminder that I am never alone.

Life has presented me with countless opportunities to witness the kindness and help of others. The generosity and compassion extended to me by friends, acquaintances, and even strangers have left an indelible mark on my heart. Their acts of selflessness have not only eased my burdens, but have also taught me the importance of paying it forwards.

Gratitude has allowed me to forge friendships that transcend time and distance; they illuminated the path for me towards resilience and strength. The appreciation I hold for these cherished bonds is immeasurable.

I am grateful for the chances I have been given, the doors that have opened, and the obstacles that have propelled me forwards. Each challenge is an opportunity for growth, and I am grateful for the resilience that emerges from such situations.

Gratitude is not just a positive attitude; it is a lifeline that keeps me afloat amidst turbulent situations.

****
Louise Phelan is a high-level strategic advisor and businesswoman. She is a strategic commercial advisor, non-executive director and ex-CEO of Phelan Energy Group and the ex-VP of PayPal.

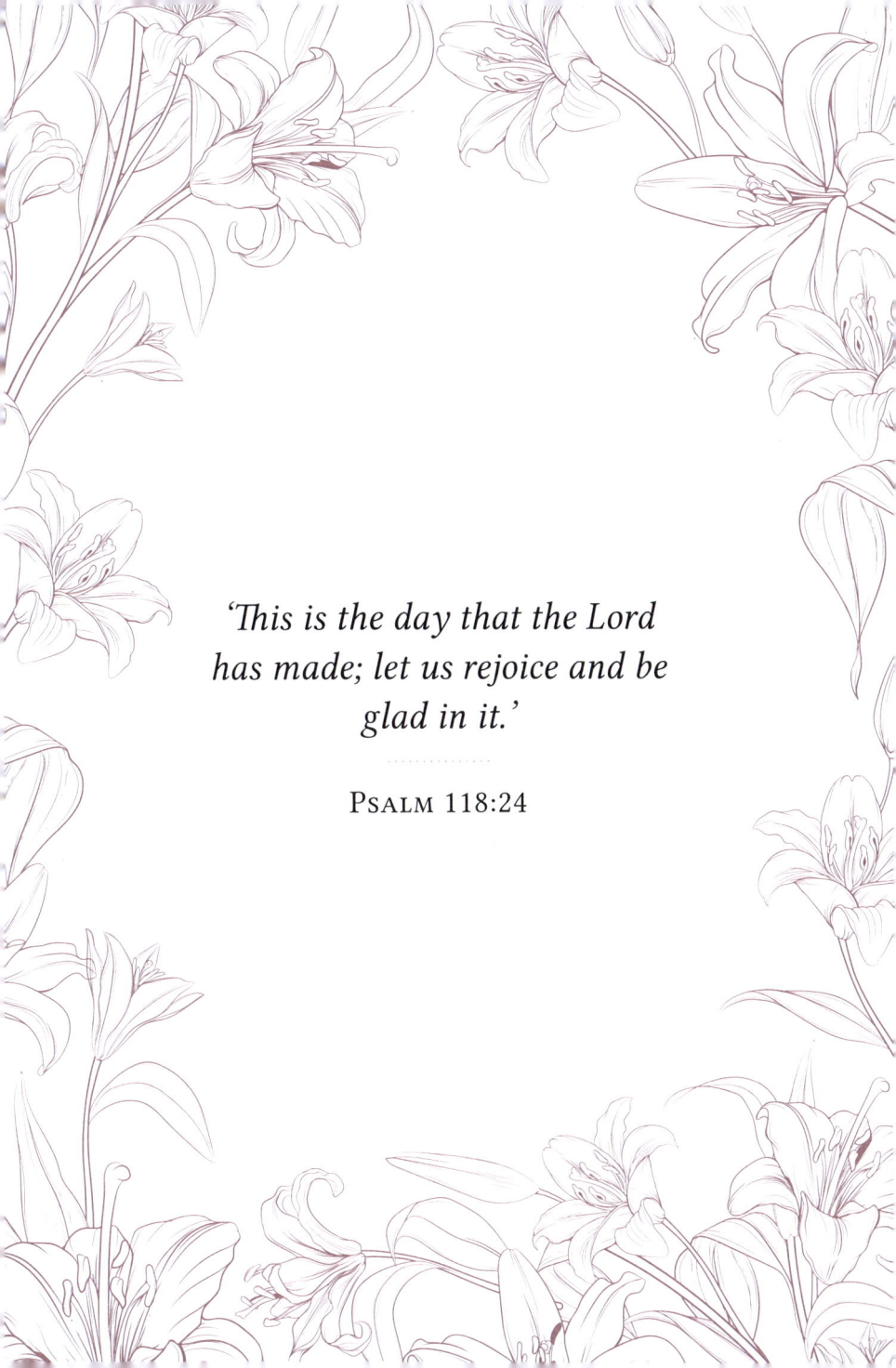

'This is the day that the Lord has made; let us rejoice and be glad in it.'

Psalm 118:24

GRATITUDE BRINGS HAPPINESS

Marie Farrell

My name is Marie and I am 45 years old. I have two beautiful girls, Nicole and Katlin. I'm from Kildare, but living in Dublin for two years. If someone asked me today what I was grateful for, this is what I would say.

The first thing I do every morning and night is say the Serenity Prayer. 'God grant me the serenity to accept the things I cannot change, the courage to change the things I can, and the wisdom to know the difference.'

This prayer has helped me to find peace in some dark days when I felt very low, and is important to me today. There was a time I didn't practice gratitude, as I took life for granted. It took a lot of pain, loss and feeling I had nothing to live for anymore to start me working on myself, and help me to look at life in a very different way. That's when I started working on gratitude and writing in my journal every day. Today, I'm grateful to wake up in the morning and try to bring some positivity to even one person I talk to. I'm grateful for getting a second chance of life; for the first time in years I love me. I'm grateful for my two beautiful girls of whom I'm so proud, and who are now proud of their mammy, for my strong bond with my family, who have stood by me and always have my back, and for the people who believed in me when I didn't.

It's the little things that some people may take for granted that I'm so grateful for: from waking up, to going to sleep at night feeling safe and warm; for having a job I love going to and feeling I'm appreciated there; to be able to walk into a church and feel the presence straight away of my own mum and dad and talk to them whenever I want; and to be able to talk to people every day and do my best to give them some glimmer of light and hope when they are in a dark place. There is a beautiful quote that I like to remind myself of: 'it's not happiness that brings gratitude, it's gratitude that brings happiness.'

I truly believe in this. The more you give out, the more you receive, as once I started to journal and kept working on myself and gave some hope to others, the more I received and continue to do so every day, as life is so short.

I will leave you with this:

Happiness cannot be travelled to, owned, earned or worn.

Happiness is the spiritual experience of living every minute with love, grace and gratitude.

Marie Farrell has been working as a peer support worker in Focus Ireland's coffee shop since September 2023. She has life experience of addiction, grief, and mental and emotional abuse, and so can relate to many of the customers. She is thankful to be given a second chance at life, and will continue to grab it with both hands.

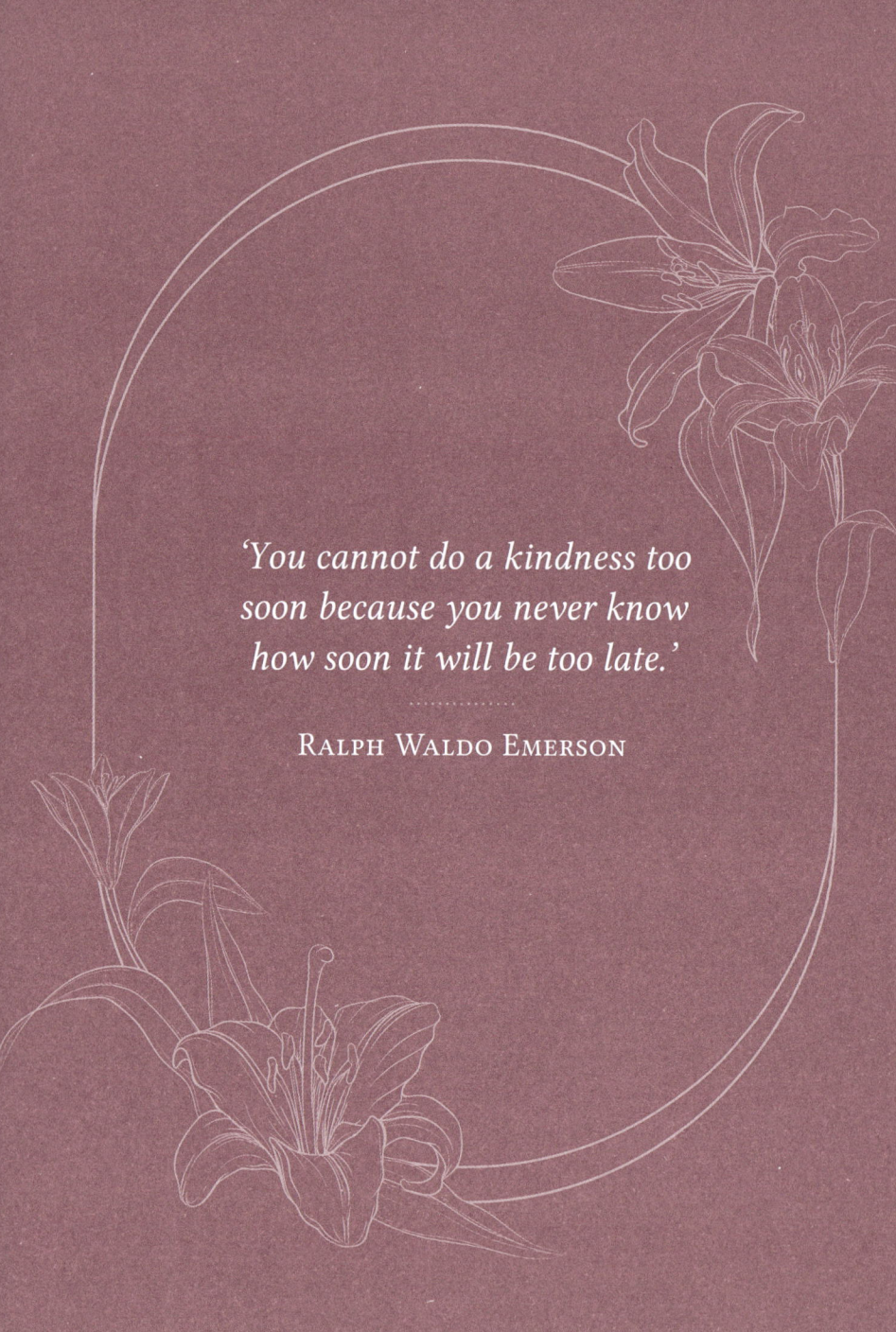

'You cannot do a kindness too soon because you never know how soon it will be too late.'

RALPH WALDO EMERSON

· GRATITUDE ·

THE GIFT OF JOY

Mary Black

As a very young girl, I remember looking at my mother's face and thinking how beautiful it was, how much I loved every line and crevice, but mostly how I knew she loved me, even though it was never really said. I'm now realising that it wasn't just love, but gratefulness that she was my mother and I was her daughter. It was around this time in childhood I started noticing how people's faces changed when they heard me sing. There was joy, and for that gift I continue to be grateful.

My father was a very proud Antrim man who was born and reared on Rathlin Island. Myself and my four siblings were reared on Charlemont Street in inner-city Dublin; however every summer we were whisked away to the wilds of Rathlin Island. So many kids on our street never left the city, but we spent weeks every summer running around the fields, milking cows, collecting eggs and baking bread with my auntie Mary. I knew even then how special this was and how lucky we were.

My mother always said, 'what's for you won't go by you', and I truly believe that meeting and marrying my husband, Joe, was meant to be. Not only did I meet a good and honest husband, but as time went on he became my manager, and record label, and grew my career with me. He continues to have my best interests at heart, and I'm truly grateful for his constant love and support.

I'm also blessed to have three well-rounded children who have grown into good, caring people of whom I am so proud. I feel very lucky that all three of them love spending time with us, and I cherish Sunday dinners when we all come together in the house they grew up in.

At present, the world seems to be full of unrest, with the Russian/Ukraine war, and the persecution of the Palestinian people by Israel. This makes me appreciate even more how after decades of war here in our country, we can live in peace. For this, I am truly grateful, and it also gives me hope that peace can be achieved between countries if the will is there.

• •

Mary Black is an Irish folk singer. She is well known as an interpreter of both traditional folk and modern material.

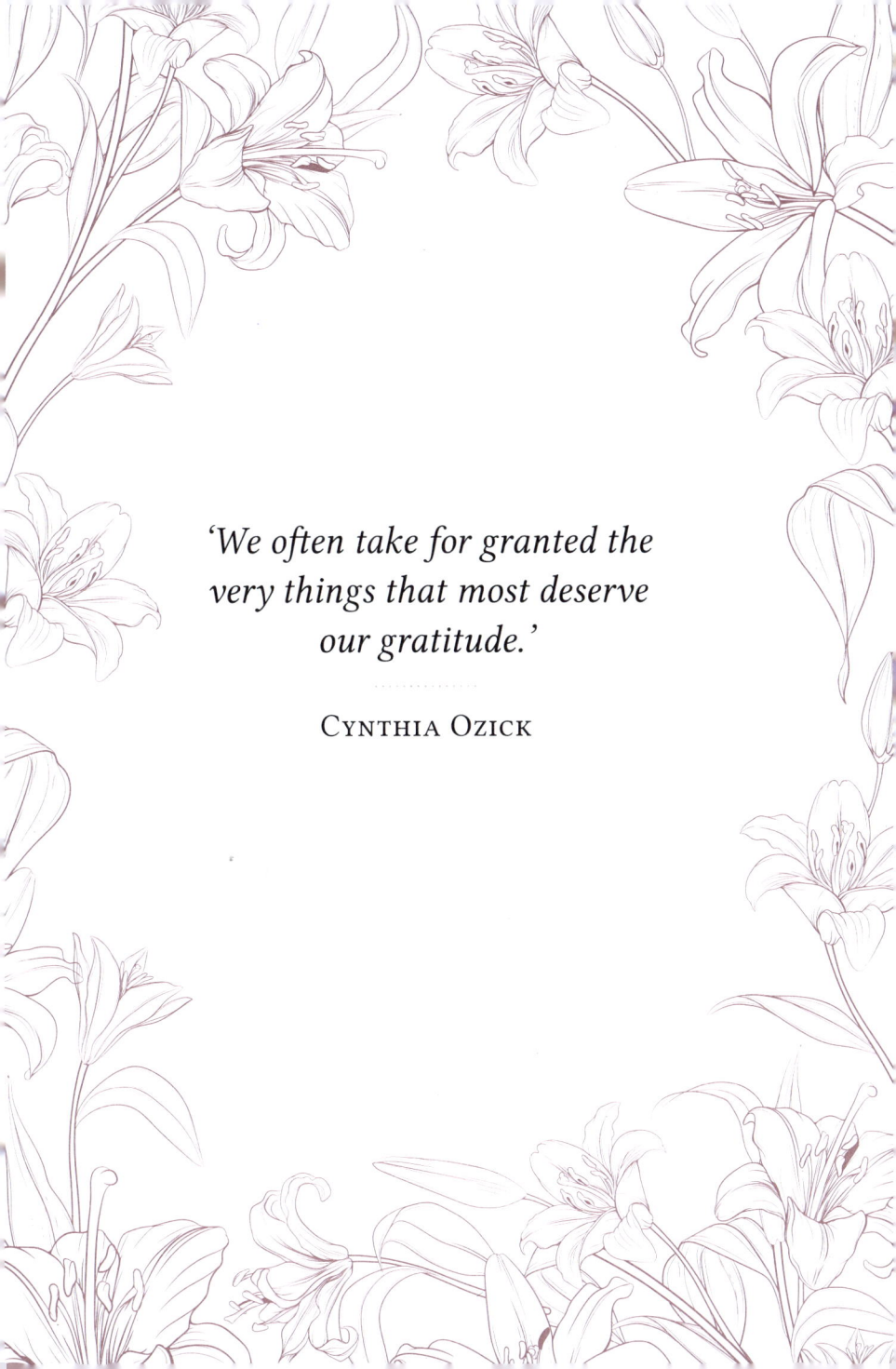

'We often take for granted the very things that most deserve our gratitude.'

Cynthia Ozick

· SR STAN ·

THE POWER OF EDUCATION
....

Mary Canning

I am grateful to my parents for giving me the opportunity not just to go to school and university, but for allowing me to choose what I wanted to study without reference to any possible material gain. These were opportunities that they had not themselves enjoyed. Every day I spent as a student in UCD was filled with debate, discovery and fun. Opportunities that now seem extraordinary came my way. Studying Italian led to a scholarship from the Italian government for a postgraduate year in Rome. Writing a PhD thesis in Anglo-Irish literature was a gruelling task which taught me research discipline and the necessity of persevering through seemingly impossible difficulties. In short, studying the humanities prepared me for critical thinking and problem-solving, as well as for standing up in front of a class of students and learning from them while, in turn, drawing out their potential to learn and to succeed.

When dark days came and personal tragedy struck, education equipped me to secure jobs to support my children, and it empowered me to create a career which evolved in ways that would have been impossible to foresee as a schoolgirl or student, and which led me to meet a life partner who supported me in every endeavour. Eventually, I was privileged to write on education policy for an international organisation, and to work with teachers and students from countries where access to the kind of opportunities my parents had given me were unattainable except for the very rich. When I sat on the floor of girls' schools in Rajasthan because there were no desks, or talked to students in Cali, Colombia, whose families had been ripped apart by the drug cartels, I certainly understood inequality. These were humbling experiences; and when the teachers, students and families of a school in Goris in rural Armenia cooked their local produce for me and we all sat down to eat it together, it tasted like some of the best food I had ever eaten, and I was moved to tears of gratitude because these people had none of this world's goods and were giving me their food for my soul.

....

Dr Mary Canning is chair of the Governing Authority of Maynooth University. She was president of the Royal Irish Academy from 2020 to 2023. She holds a D.Litt. honoris causa from NUI, and has served on numerous boards in Ireland since her retirement. Previously, she was lead education specialist in the World Bank in Washington DC.

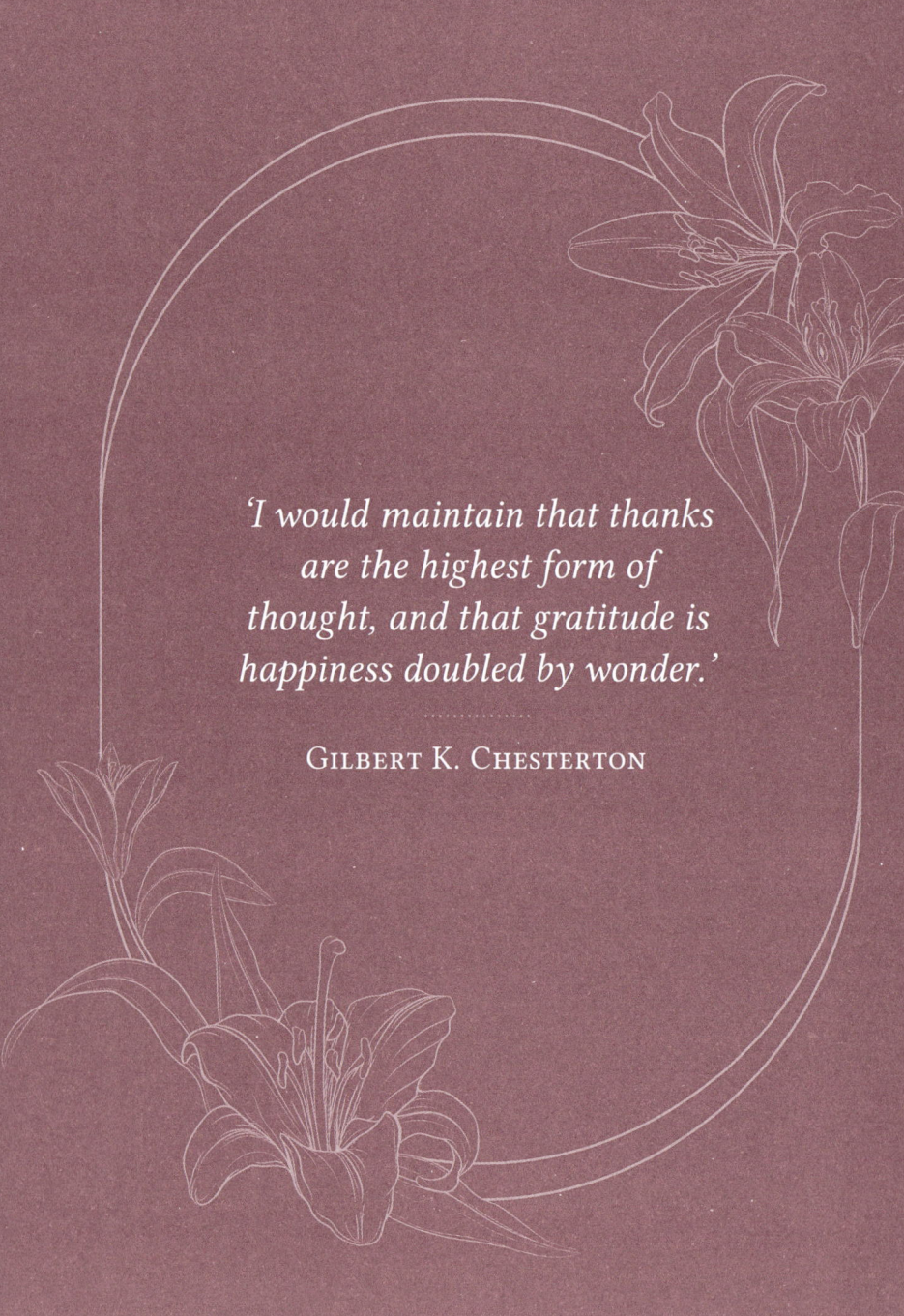

'I would maintain that thanks are the highest form of thought, and that gratitude is happiness doubled by wonder.'

Gilbert K. Chesterton

· GRATITUDE ·

TAKING A MINUTE

Mary Coughlan

Some days I have moments of sublime happiness!
I usually stop my car at the bottom of the laneway that leads up to the Little Sugar Loaf and take a minute to:

Be grateful for where I live.
The light on the trees. The gorse is so yellow this time of year, and the birds are singing.
I often stand outside at night and look at the stars,
Bathe in the light of the moon,
Feel the ground beneath my feet.

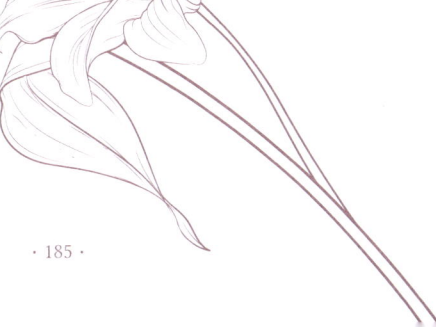

· SR STAN ·

I feel grateful:
For my family,
My friends,
My voice, my music and for all the people I work with;
For the opportunities I've had to travel the Earth.
I'm grateful for my sobriety,
For this life I've been given;
So grateful for being
Alive.

> Mary Coughlan, born in Galway in 1956, has made some of the most personal and universal music of any Irish artist. She has five children and six grandchildren. She was twice married and divorced, and has one in training.

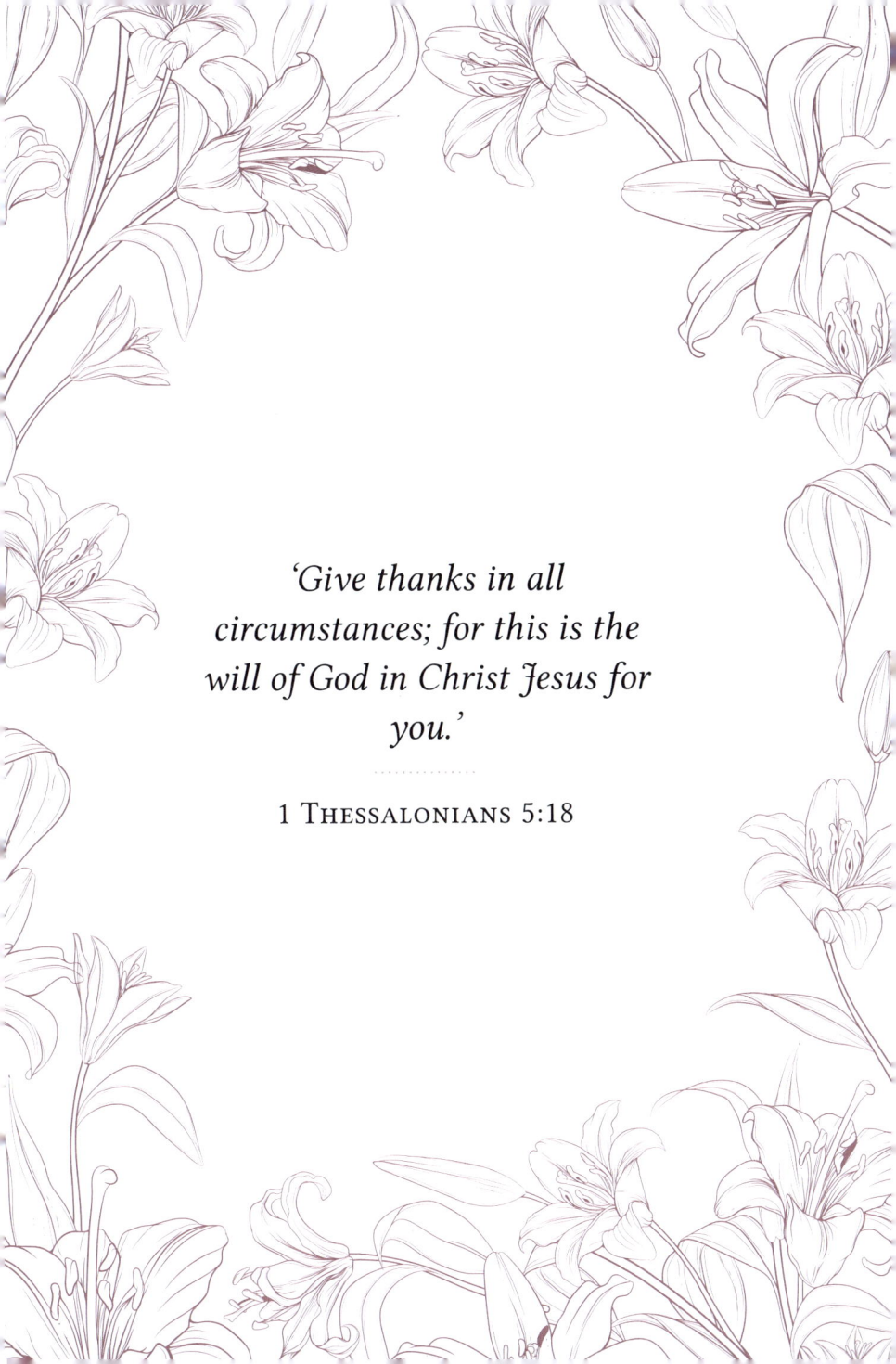

'Give thanks in all circumstances; for this is the will of God in Christ Jesus for you.'

1 Thessalonians 5:18

LOOKING FOR THE POSITIVE

Mary Hunt

'We've a lot to be thankful for' was something my mother used to say. It was her way of showing gratitude. 'Thanks be to God' is another lovely phrase used by Irish people. God, the giver of all we are and have, is the one to whom we should indeed be grateful.

It's raining today. We could complain, but wouldn't it be better to give thanks for our green fields and constant supply of water? With our gratitude comes acceptance of God's will and wisdom. In our gratitude, we can see the usefulness of the rain. If humans had their own way, the world might not work in the mysterious and wonderful way it does. God is full of wisdom. Creation is his great gift. He knows how things work for our good. In my personal life, I have many reasons to be grateful. First and foremost, for my parents, especially my mother, with whom I was very close. Also, my sisters who love me, my nieces and nephew, and all family and friends. I'm grateful to my partner, David, for the sense of security he provides. Despite his disability, he is great fun and very kind. I suffer from schizophrenia; not a very nice condition. I could look at the negative, which I can assure you is very real, or I could focus on all that is good. I lived in social housing for ten years. I am eternally grateful to those who set up and ran the house. I attended a training course with the now National Learning Network, and even though I was unwell at the time, managed to work with the NLN for two years. I became too unwell to work, and that time was difficult, but there were positives, and I'm sure I did some good. I'm grateful for the training and encouragement I received then. I'm grateful also to God for blessing me with creative gifts.

When I think like this, it colours my view of the world in a good way. It's easy to focus on the negative; our brains are wired that way. Being positive takes effort. Gratitude for all that is right and good in our lives promotes a positive outlook. It would not be wise to deny that negative things happen. They do. However, looking for the positive in a situation really works. Thanks be to God.

Mary Hunt is from Strokestown in Co. Roscommon. She loves to write and paint. She is an occasional writer for the Messenger *magazine.*

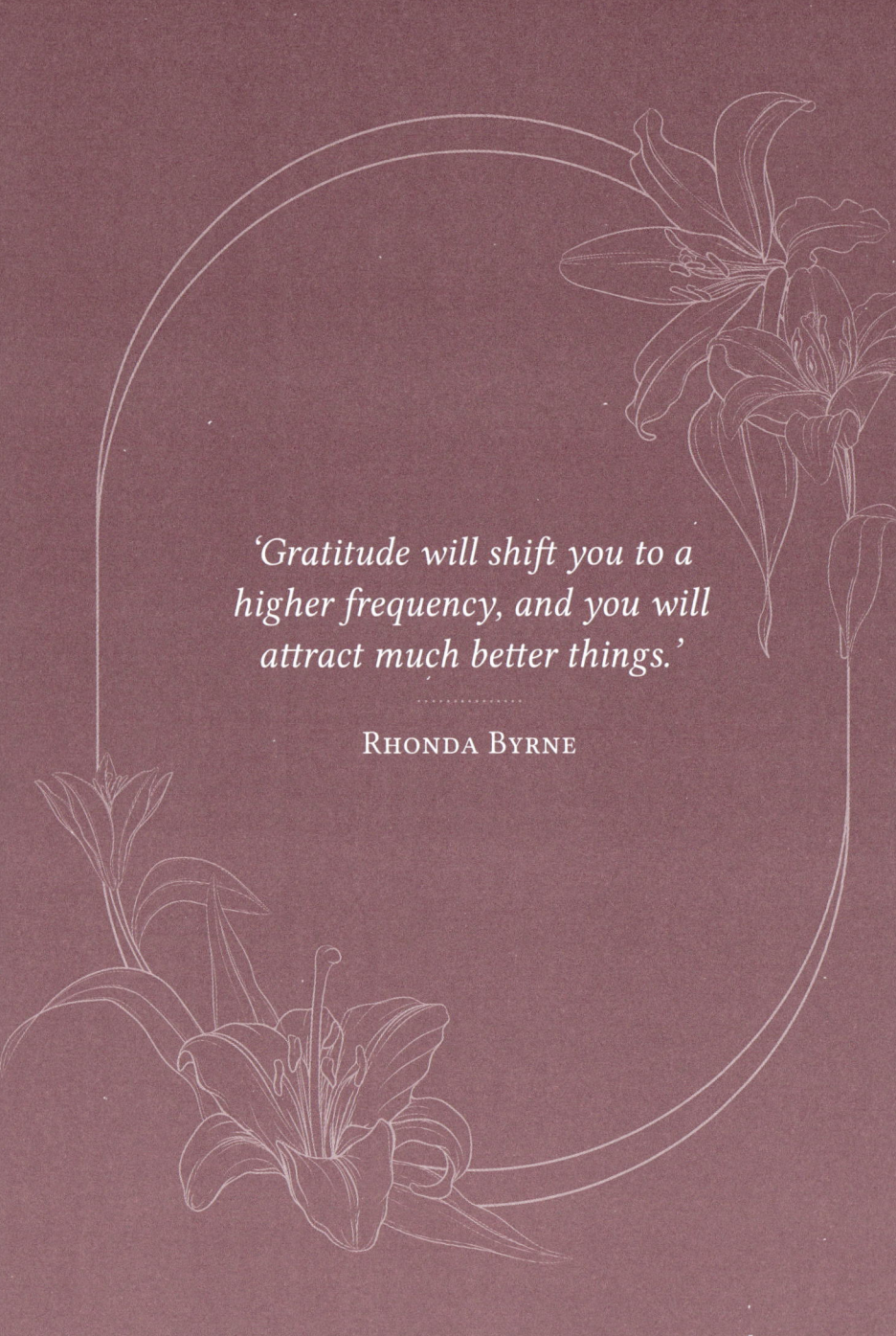

'Gratitude will shift you to a higher frequency, and you will attract much better things.'

RHONDA BYRNE

· GRATITUDE ·

SAYING THANK YOU

Matt Cooper

Saying 'thank you' might seem like a relatively small thing, but saying it means something to me and hopefully to those to whom I say it.

It's not just a matter of good manners. I associate those simple words with gratitude. Saying 'thank you' is a simple way of expressing gratitude on all those occasions when, without the input of others, I wouldn't be able to do what I need to do.

For example, I finish my radio show each evening by thanking each member of my production team on air by name. I may be the person who is heard on air, interviewing others, but I wouldn't have those guests if it wasn't for my team booking the people to be available at the required times. They also provide me with talking points for the interviews. I have to thank them because I wouldn't be able to do my job without them.

I also thank the sound engineer, because nobody would hear me without his work.

I thank the guests for joining me and the listeners, even if the interview has been fraught, as sometimes they are.

Hopefully I remember to do that on every interaction I have – with those who might serve me food in a restaurant or coffee in a café; with the taxi driver who drops me off, or even the bus driver who has moved me safely from one point to another.

People can become islands, remote from each other, so I'm grateful that others – my family, my friends, my workmates and many more – are willing to interact with me.

So thank you for that.

....

Matt Cooper presents The Last Word *on Today FM and writes for newspapers.*

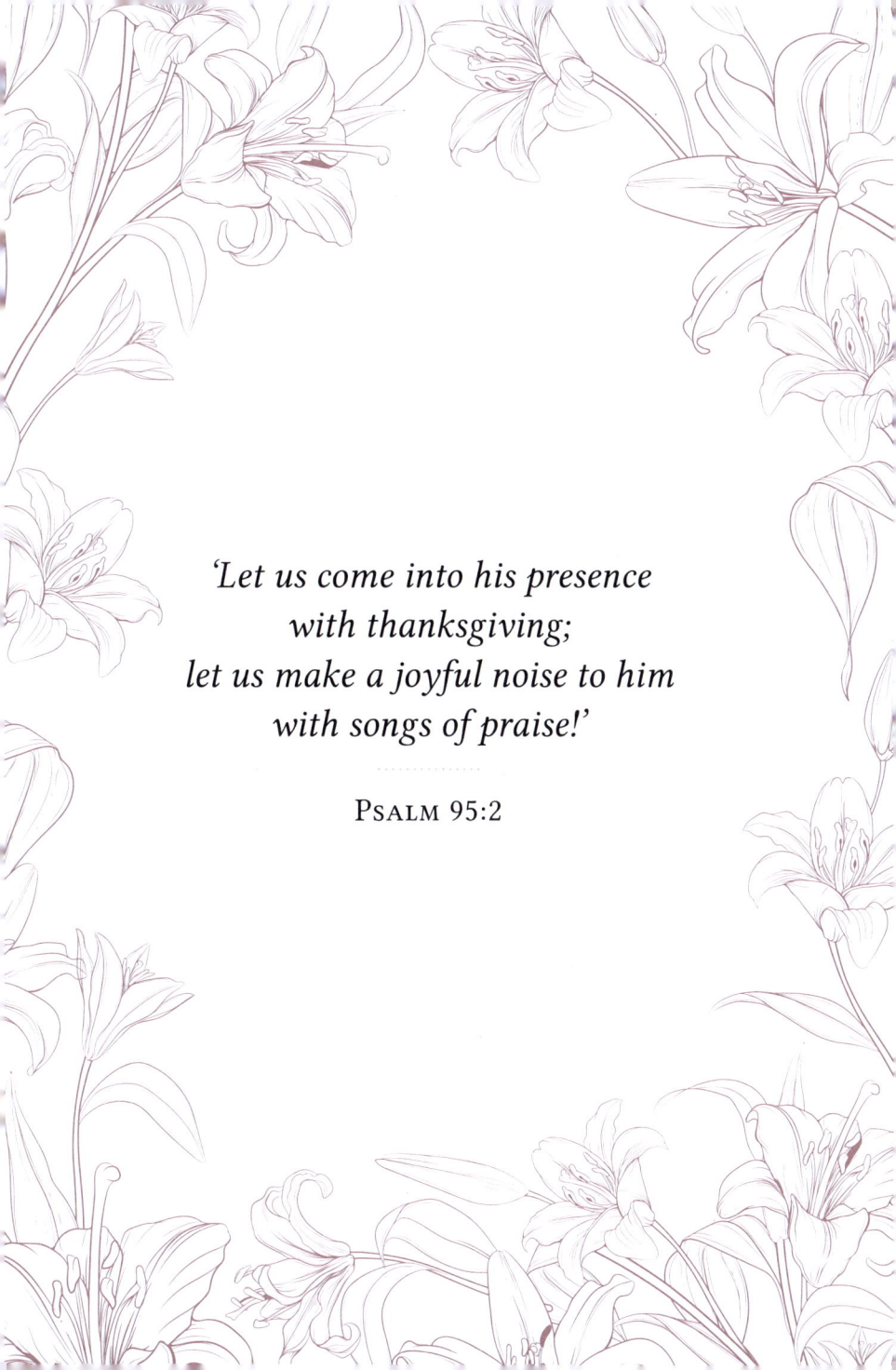

'Let us come into his presence
with thanksgiving;
let us make a joyful noise to him
with songs of praise!'

Psalm 95:2

THE POTENTIAL OF HOPE

Michelle O'Neill

When we find ourselves at a particularly important juncture in life, it's important to stop, and reflect to remind ourselves how far we have come, and the journey that still stretches out ahead of us.

In the whirlwind of recent developments which saw me become First Minister in the North, I stood back for a few minutes from the intensity of new pressures and demands to simply stop and think about the enormity of what had happened, and to remember and appreciate those who helped bring us to this point.

To me, that is what gratitude is – taking time to be thankful for what we have been given, and the potential of what that may bring.

As someone born into what seemed an intractable conflict, I am particularly thankful for the achievements of our peace process, and grateful to those who took the courageous steps necessary to bring us out of conflict.

We have come an incredibly long way as a society over the past three decades.

We should never forget that, even though it can be tempting to take the achievements of the peace process

· GRATITUDE ·

for granted and become frustrated at what, at times, can be the slow pace of change.

I have every sympathy with that. I am impatient for change. I am impatient for the creation of a better, brighter future for everyone on the island of Ireland.

But I also recognise, and have deep gratitude for, the huge changes that have already taken place for the better across this society.

I see the strides towards equality and the eradication of the discrimination and injustice in the North that previous generations had to endure, and the social and economic progress and potential for equality and prosperity across the island.

As the first nationalist and republican First Minister, my appointment is evidence of that progress and change.

When I look around the North today, I see a society that has been transformed. I see a generation of young people full of hope, not hatred, and I see a peace and political process that is an example for conflict resolution around the world.

In today's world, that is more important than ever.

Because, while we are thankful for our peace process, it is also a source of hope for others.

In these darkest of times for the besieged people of Gaza and Palestine, we can offer support and solidarity; but I sincerely believe that we can also offer hope that, through ceasefire, dialogue and negotiation, their nightmare can be brought to an end.

For my generation and those generations that follow, I want to express gratitude to those who helped bring us out of a long and painful history, and to a better, peaceful Ireland.

> Michelle O'Neill was appointed First Minister in the Stormont Assembly in February 2024. She has been Sinn Féin Vice President since 2018. Michelle was elected as Assembly member in 2007, and has been the MLA for the Mid-Ulster constituency since then, and was deputy First Minister from 2020 to 2022.

'Our enemies provide us with a precious opportunity to practice patience and love. We should have gratitude toward them.'

Dalai Lama

SR STAN

USING THE TOOLS YOU HAVE

Mick Clifford

Soon after our firstborn came into the world, I had a little moment. We were sitting in the family car outside the National Botanic Gardens in Dublin. My partner was feeding our son in the back seat. I was behind the wheel, inactive, waiting for the business to end so we could move off. Then, out of nowhere, I felt captured in a warm, fuzzy bubble. It lasted no more than ten or so seconds, but for that fleeting period there was no world outside our little capsule on wheels. There was no past or future, no worry or stress. There was nothing else, good, bad or indifferent, occupying my mind. Everything was there in the moment, our own little perfect world with this human bundle still wrapped in mystery. The feeling wasn't one of joy or ecstasy, just complete contentment, warmth. I'm grateful that I can still remember that moment, and reach back to it whenever life's harder moments require addressing.

I'm grateful for my capacity to recognise my luck. That is something I have learned over the years. For a long time, I didn't even consider that I was lucky, failing to understand that the slings and arrows of life are unavoidable; it is the tools with which we are equipped to tackle them that makes the difference; and fate allocates those tools, to the greatest extent, randomly. I'm grateful that my number came up in that respect.

I'm grateful for the mornings when I come downstairs in the dark and see a new day about to take shape, knowing that I will have the privilege of living it without any of the serious challenges so many face on a daily basis, in this country and in places where human potential is not, and may never be, realised to the extent that it is here. I'm grateful for experiencing all the small things that constitute living today. That is as it is now. Who knows what tomorrow brings and whether my luck will change. If, and more likely, when it does, I can only hope I have the wherewithal to continue being grateful for all I've experienced, and with whom I've experienced it.

Mick Clifford is a reporter and columnist with the Irish Examiner. *He has been a journalist for thirty years, and is the author of five books and co-author of three more. He also presents a weekly podcast for the* Irish Examiner.

'Let us rise up and be thankful, for if we didn't learn a lot today, at least we learned a little, and if we didn't learn a little, at least we didn't get sick, and if we got sick, at least we didn't die; so, let us all be thankful.'

BUDDHA

GRATITUDE EMPOWERS

Monica McWilliams

Gratitude, as I know it, comes in so many different ways. From an early age, my mother would say, 'don't forget to write and say thank you.' This was for a gift or a kindness. Later, I learned to show gratitude to anyone imparting their skills, not knowing what a difference they were making to my thinking – personally and politically. These 'influencers' and 'mentors' didn't have to prove how clever they were. It was their generosity along with their wisdom that impressed me the most, and I am especially grateful to the women who were at my side as we struggled to get our voices heard during the peace process in Northern Ireland.

When the Women's Coalition stood for election to the peace negotiations in 1996, one of my tasks was to do the 'cold calling', which meant picking up the phone and asking for funds for a women's political party. To show my gratitude afterwards, I sent a signed copy of the Good Friday Agreement to each of our supporters – at home and abroad. I was struck by their response: 'Thank *you* for asking me to help.' I later learned that it wasn't just kindness; they felt included, as it gave them a sense of belonging to something important – even if we didn't know that at the time.

I frequently respond to requests from event organisers or from students and journalists for interviews with, 'Thanks for the invite.' But when I give my time – even late at night – so many of them never get back to me. The exception makes it even more gratifying when I get a note or a card to say how much it was appreciated; and to the person who didn't show gratitude, you won't get me to come back again.

When I was a student in the USA, my standard response if I was praised or shown gratitude – for a talk I gave or for what I was wearing – took the form of, 'Ah, sure that's nothing.' But paying a compliment for something I had achieved deserved a different response. Their gratitude was to encourage me – providing confidence and self-esteem, especially in a culture where women and girls are unaccustomed to it. To give and receive gratitude is empowering, and I do it now every chance I get.

Monica McWilliams represented the Northern Ireland Women's Coalition at the multi-party peace talks, and is a signatory to the Good Friday Agreement. She currently works with women in other conflict regions, and her recent memoir, Stand Up, Speak Out, *tells the story of her activism in various social movements.*

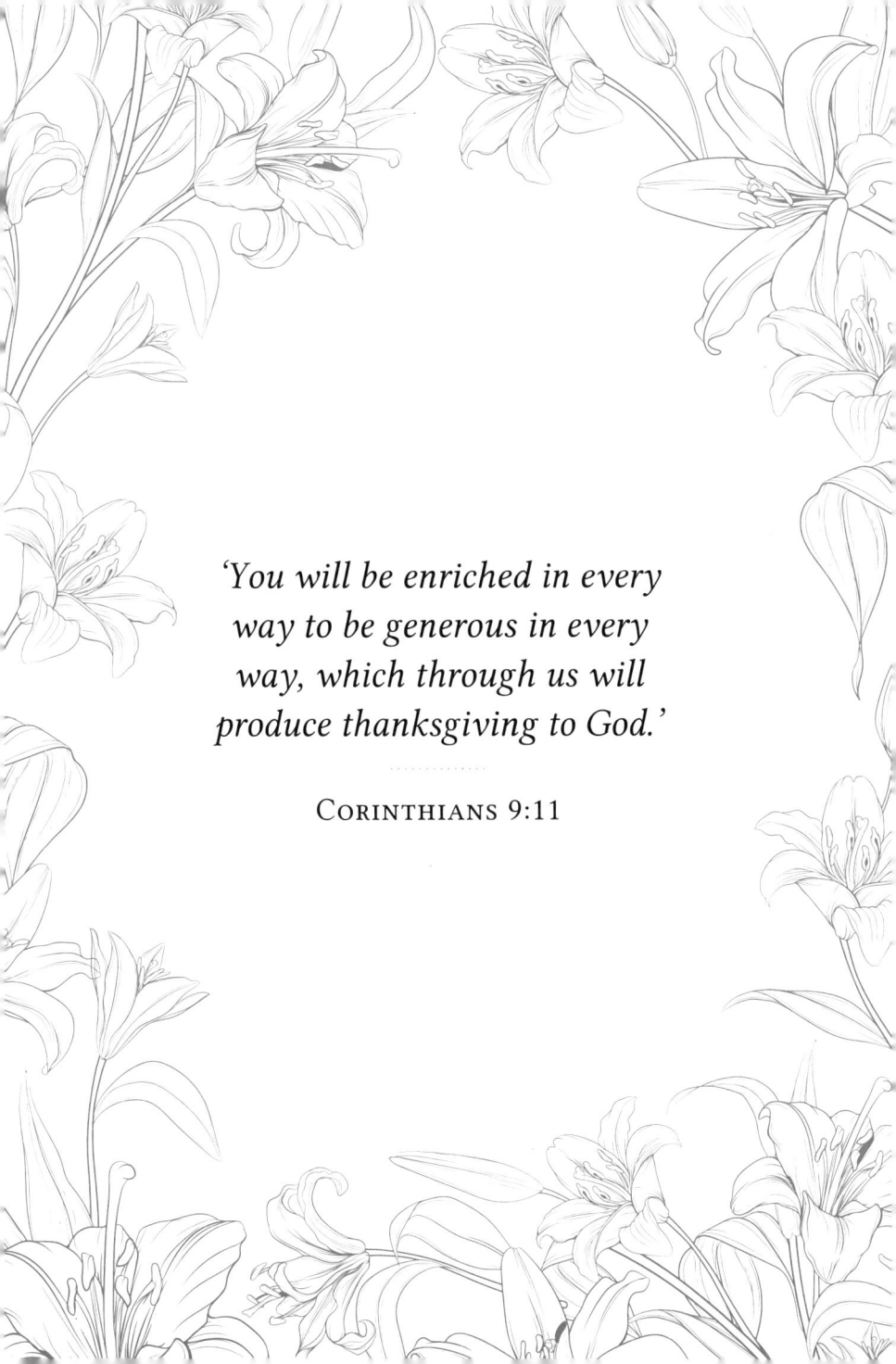

'You will be enriched in every way to be generous in every way, which through us will produce thanksgiving to God.'

Corinthians 9:11

GROUNDING

Niall Muldoon

As Ombudsman for Children, I get to see the huge challenges that many children face on a daily basis, and I believe that gratitude is more important now than ever before. I was lucky to be born and bred in south Donegal into a great family with two brothers and one sister. While we never really spoke about gratitude as a concept, my father was religious and my mother also has a strong belief in the strength of a higher power, and, because of that, I think we were always aware of the need to 'give thanks'. As young kids, between 6 p.m. and 7 p.m., we would get a call to come in from wherever we were playing to say the Rosary – a very quaint notion now that most children would not even be aware of, never mind understand. However, that time was family time and ringfenced for us to be together and give our thanks to a higher power.

I will always be thankful for that grounding from my parents. They allowed me to see the importance of recognising that what we have, both materially and emotionally, may be connected with forces/elements outside of ourselves. I have always believed in my own personal efforts being hugely important in shaping the direction of my life, but I have never considered them to be the only factor.

I think seeing outside of yourself at how life might be shaped by fate/a higher power/Budda/God/etc. allows humility, and generates a recognition that just because you want it badly enough, that does not mean you will get it. I see that as a very human understanding, and something that leads me to be grateful when I *do* get something I might wish for.

Therefore, it gives me great comfort to accept that not everything is under my control, and so I have generated a habit of expressing my gratefulness for two things in my life – the first is the good things I (and my family) have, and the second is the bad things we do *not* have. That is the mantra I will deliver as I begin to drift off to sleep on many nights – not all nights, but regularly.

Niall Muldoon is the Ombudsman for Children.

'Gratitude helps you to grow and expand; gratitude brings joy and laughter into your life and into the lives of all those around you.'

EILEEN CADDY

FINDING ROOM FOR GRATITUDE IN THE QUEST TO SUCCEED

Niall Quinn

Looking back on a football life of early struggle and eventual privilege, I realise that discovering the power of gratitude made my journey a happier one.

I didn't always understand its power, but now I know that gratitude's calming energy put brakes on my irrational desire to achieve at all costs. It took me a while to appreciate what I had, as opposed to what I lacked.

Embracing the power of gratitude served to mute this harmful preoccupation, and quickly led me to a happier place where my football actually flourished.

'Count your blessings, not your problems.'

Sounds easy now, but for a period in my development I was not listening. I was caught up in a harmful desire to succeed no matter what, but afraid and haunted by the fear of failure and becoming a let-down.

I understand now that while it's ok to be an ambitious teenager, setting out to achieve goals at all costs, while smothering in fear of failure and ignoring those around you offering help, is a fast track to nowhere.

As a young trainee at Arsenal, I was consumed by the pressure to succeed. I was drowning in negative self-analysis, I was deaf to any supports, and made little progress in the first eighteen months.

Then something changed. A new coach, a new voice – ex-Irish player Pat Rice came in and brought his influence into my world. His selfless dedication to making me a better person before making me a better player lifted me to a new level.

'Remember who you are, where you are and whom you represent.'
'Always be grateful that you are paid to do something you love.'
'Your worst day could be the best day of an Arsenal fan's life.'

Understanding the help that I was getting from Pat matured me, I've no doubt about that. Playing professional football and 'making it' went from being a colossal burden to a joyous pursuit, and to this day I implore young players to find room for gratitude in their quest to succeed, just as I did.

What do I say to them? Be thankful for who you are, where you are and to those you represent, and don't get sidetracked by other people's perceived glories – as Pat Rice told us many's the time.

'Comparison is the thief of joy.'

That says it all really. Thanks, Pat.

· ·

Niall Quinn is an Irish former professional footballer, manager, businessman and sports television pundit. He played for Arsenal, Manchester City and Sunderland, and also received 92 caps for the Republic of Ireland national football team, scoring 21 times, which makes him Ireland's second-highest goal-scorer of all time.

'*A generous heart, kind speech, and a life of service and compassion are the things which renew humanity.*'

GAUTAMA BUDDHA

BUILDING A WARM WELCOME

Niamh McDonald

No matter who you are, where you come from or how you identify, if you arrived yesterday or have lived in Ireland all your life, you deserve to have a safe, secure, warm home and a safe community that meets your needs so everyone can flourish.

I lead an organisation called the Hope and Courage Collective (H&CC). Our mission is to disrupt far-right hate and fascism through advocacy, analysis and communications, and by developing a powerful ecosystem supporting resilient communities, workplaces, public institutions and democracy.

H&CC is part of a wider ecosystem of responses, as disinformation, fear, anger and mistrust seep into Irish society. It will take community leaders from all walks of life to stand up and reject hate and fear, while maintaining welcoming communities, and fighting for the material needs of everyone who lives in them.

H&CC acts as a catalyst, bringing together groups of people who may have never had to work together before. We work with people directly affected by hate and extremism, and community leaders responding to hate on the ground. People from all parts of the island, day in, day out are bravely standing up to lies, hate and violence, while building community solidarity.

I feel a deep sense of gratitude when people come together and commit to ensuring their towns and villages continue to be places of welcome, and are able to provide support for all who live there. This gratitude creates the nourishment and hope needed to do this role.

I am also hugely grateful for so many leaders across civil society, be it those in a local village or in national organisations. I am inspired by their commitment and resolve to build a shared response, and to work together to ensure the forces of hate do not row back on the gains already made or prevent much needed progress.

The extremists know the more we progress towards equity for all, the less space there is for hate and fascism.

Niamh McDonald is the director of the Hope and Courage Collective. Niamh has over 15 years of experience in community organising and campaigning. She is a member of SPARK (Single Parents Acting for the Rights of their Kids) and is a graduate of Maynooth University with a bachelor's degree in social sciences.

'Gratitude is the sweetest thing
in a seeker's life
in all human life. If there is
gratitude in your heart, then
there will be tremendous
sweetness in your eyes.'

SRI CHINMOY

GRATITUDE CORNER

Noel Cunningham

Gratitude. I never knew truthfully what this word meant. So often, I said I am so grateful ... So often, I thought I was grateful ... So often, I thought gratitude played a big part in my life! How wrong one can be. I never knew the true meaning or sense of gratitude until life decided a few harsh lessons were to be included in my book of chance. The path towards appreciating and understanding gratitude would lie at the end of a rather rocky road. There are many who battle addiction. My addiction crept up on me. With hindsight, I now know that there are reasons for my addiction. A young lad in a rural setting, trying to be something he wasn't, and fighting the inevitability of being gay. This left me vulnerable and hurt. I travelled aimlessly, moved homes and jobs without any peace, contentment or happiness in life. Geographical moves were not the answer.

Amazingly, I never lost hope. It was the death of my sister and her husband in a horrific car accident, and the words spoken by their beautiful young daughter, that put me on that road that led me back to what I call my gratitude corner. My beloved niece told me very bluntly that I had to give up drink, and I did. With the help of Alcoholics Anonymous, I managed to get my life back on track.

What followed was new achievements. I built a career and found so many positive blessings that I cannot count without feeling overwhelmed with gratitude. I managed, having lost everything, to get a roof over my head, a car and respect, particularly from my family. I had squandered so much, I had to make amends.

Now I wake in the morning knowing that I have a contribution to make in life. I know I can give something back. I know I can make a difference, and I say with pride that I thank my God in every way for the journey I've made and the destination I've reached. That destination is my gratitude corner, and I am very fortunate in my work that I have been able to speak about my journey of addiction, and to try to explain my fulsome heart, and the joy and gratitude that I have in my heart. That gratitude extends to trying to get people who are addicts to realise that they can too find their gratitude corners. My journey can inspire them to try to pick up the pieces of their fractured lives. My gratitude extends to being sober, and being able to have that national platform to talk from and allow people to see me at my most vulnerable, but also at my most grateful. How lucky am I? Thank you, thank you, thank you.

* *

Noel Cunningham has a long and distinguished career in hotel catering and tourism, and is a well-known TV personality and author.

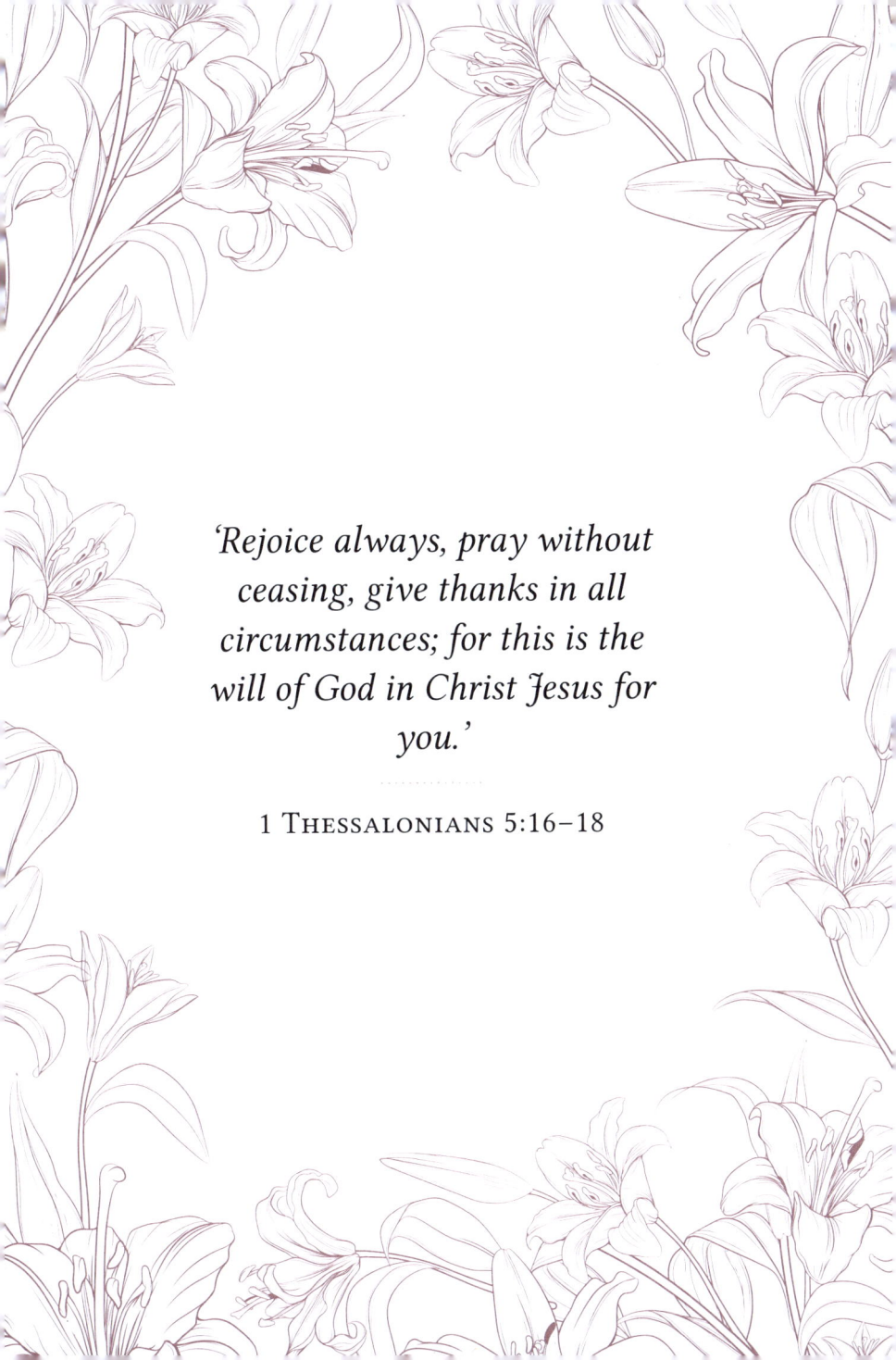

'Rejoice always, pray without ceasing, give thanks in all circumstances; for this is the will of God in Christ Jesus for you.'

1 Thessalonians 5:16–18

… SR STAN …

REAP WHAT YOU SOW

Norma Smurfit

We can often complicate what we are grateful for. It is clear to me that family and friends are what I am most grateful for. The intergenerational energy and power of engaging with my grandchildren and young people are really powerful. You will reap what you sow in life when it comes to family and friends – also, don't be afraid to make new friends in your life as you get older.

I have always been grateful for the opportunity to learn new things – I am grateful that I am open to new information and new ideas. I am also grateful for the opportunity to make a change and a difference in society; we all have the ability to make a difference.

I have found that travelling and having new experiences gives you energy and the desire to do new things, and find new ways of making a difference. We are so lucky to live in a world where the advances in science are improving the lives of

· GRATITUDE ·

so many – I am grateful that there are people who have access to education and the opportunity to do the research that allows these advances to be made.

Always nurture the thirst for knowledge, and always be ready to listen and even change your mind – I am grateful that I have the ability to do this.

I am also grateful for the opportunities I have had to enjoy the good things in life.

In summary, you should always try to be grateful, take the time to be grateful, and, as I said at the outset, the love and loyalty of family and friends is the most important of all. Gratitude is great!

Norma Smurfit has founded, supported and been involved with numerous organisations, including the Irish Youth Foundation, First Step, and the Irish Famine Commemoration Fund.

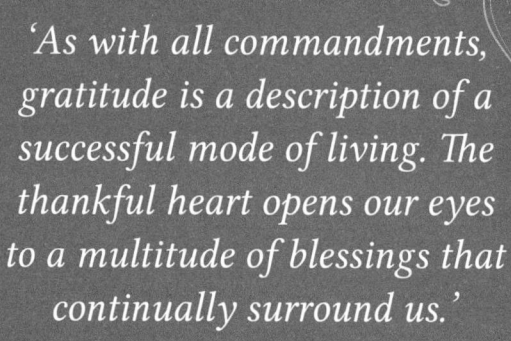

'As with all commandments, gratitude is a description of a successful mode of living. The thankful heart opens our eyes to a multitude of blessings that continually surround us.'

JAMES E. FAUST

· GRATITUDE ·

WHAT MAKES ME FEEL GRATITUDE?

Oisín Coghlan

Looking back, I had an extremely untroubled childhood, in a loving and supportive family. The older I get and the more I experience the messy challenges of everyday life, and see the reactionary forces ripping through so many families around the world, from those cornered in Gaza, or those pushed to take their chances in the Mediterranean, to those sleeping in tents on the streets of Dublin, the more grateful I feel for what I experienced as ordinary life, but was in fact extraordinary privilege.

Many people working on climate change suffer anxiety, burnout and even despair, and every life comes with setbacks, insecurities and potential crises. But by virtue of some genetic or biochemical chance, no matter how down I may occasionally feel at the end of a given day, I almost always wake up with the desire to get stuck in again. Having taken this for granted most of my life, I have come to recognise it as an unearned blessing for which I am hugely grateful.

For an environmentalist, I used to pay little attention to nature! But the pandemic lockdowns slowed me down enough to appreciate the changing seasons on the two-kilometre loops near where I live.

And, of course, my family, who drive me mad and keep me sane, love me unconditionally but don't take me too seriously, who make me laugh and occasionally even laugh at my dad jokes.

Finally, I am so grateful for my fellow activists. In the words of the US commentator David Roberts:

> When we ask for hope, I think we're just asking for fellowship. The weight of climate change, like any weight, is easier to bear with others. They are out there, men and women of extraordinary imagination, courage, and perseverance, pouring themselves into this fight for a better future. You are not alone. And as long as you are not alone, there is always hope.

* * *

Oisín Coghlan is chief executive of Friends of the Earth.

'Everyday, think as you wake up, today I am fortunate to be alive, I have a precious human life, I am not going to waste it.'

Dalai Lama

· SR STAN ·

MOMENTS OF CONNECTION

Paschal Donohoe

That moment when the needle of a record player fitted into the groove of a vinyl record was a teenage moment of magic for me. Static, with a slight looping pulse, filled the living room of my family home. And then – the music.

Back then, my tastes were far more wide-ranging than they are now; a learned and kind uncle introduced me to the world of opera, a neighbour demanded I listen to Led Zeppelin.

The Four of Us and Transvision Vamp played the tunes of teenage life.

Now, there is no record player, no removal of dust from the vinyl grooves. A universe of music is instantly available from my phone.

But that moment before a performance begins, and then the early moments of a song or aria, are still constant sources of gratitude for me; gratitude as some part of me tries to connect with some part of someone else on instruments that I cannot play, with notes that I do not understand, all of which create a language that I do not speak and cannot sing but still understand. It is just magic.

So, I offer thanks for those moments of connection.

I thank my young adult children for their world of music. Without them Olivia Rodrigo or Billie Eilish would be unknown to me. How much poorer would I be?

· GRATITUDE ·

Similarly, I offer thanks to my friend who insisted I attend an opera performance. I am now beginning to appreciate the swooning glory of Puccini. Wagner is still too much, but my future feels lusher because I know he is waiting for me.

As the years go by, these sources of gratitude also teach me something about the nature of gratitude. The 'big reveal' of joy and instant happiness rarely happens. A sudden surge of gratitude can happen, but not as frequently as you might expect.

The accumulation of melodies within the heart is gradual, and does not yield to the disappointment of a bad album or a poor gig. Similarly, the steady collection of gratitude on a daily basis is vital.

It creates the resilience for a busy life, and helps with the smile that also sets the tone of the day.

....

Paschal Donohoe is an Irish Fine Gael politician who currently serves as Minister for Public Expenditure, National Development Plan Delivery and Reform.

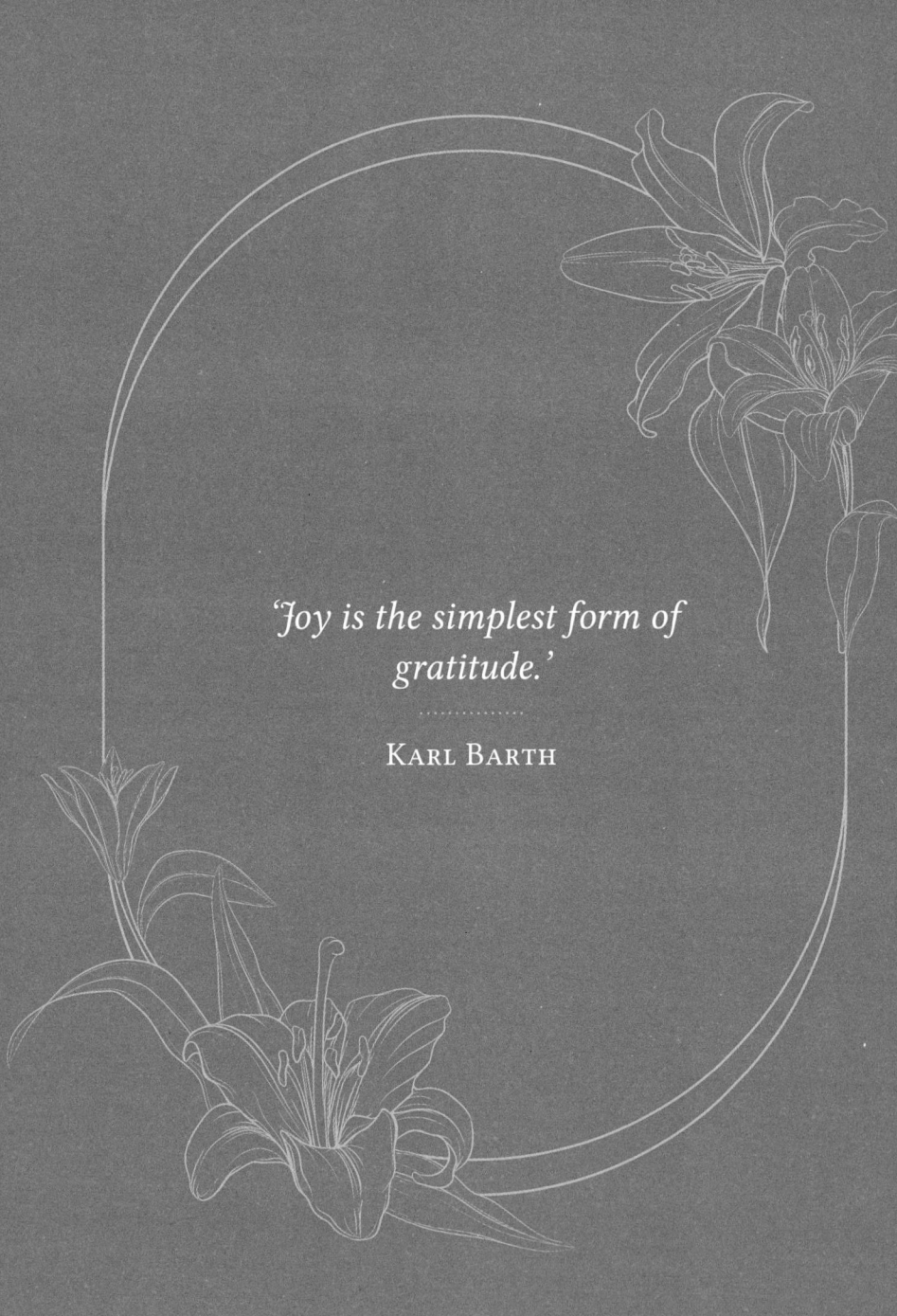

'Joy is the simplest form of gratitude.'

KARL BARTH

· GRATITUDE ·

HEDGE SCHOOL

Pat Boran

As a schoolkid, I wasn't much impressed by Poetry with a capital P. Who could be bothered with all those puzzling rules, the archaic terminology? Yet I loved a handful of rhymes and verses, many of them concerned with things already familiar – birds and animals, plants and trees, a variety of activities caught in an almost magical light, as if for the mind's eye to play back in hypnotic slow motion.

The intimate nature of these invariably small clusters of words had a profound effect on me, though it took me a long time to realise it. It turns out that by putting their faith in detail rather than in what we might call 'the bigger picture', the writers of those short songs and word sketches were trying to *show* us the world, rather than merely to *tell us about it*. In that respect, their impulse had more to do with praise, gratitude and celebration than with any literary ambition.

When Covid arrived, like a lot of people, I made a real effort to get away from my desk, even taking to writing 'on the hoof' – walking in the woods, masked-queueing at the supermarket, or just pottering around in our small back garden, grateful to have a place from which to observe the scudding clouds and changing light.

The limited radius of those months was arguably less punishing for artists and writers (and gardeners and yoga practitioners for that matter), for whom a strong connection with place is essential to the practice. Even so, in my case it brought me back to my first attempts at making poems of my own, watching the fascinating carry-on of nesting birds beyond our back door in Portlaoise in the early 1970s.

Fifty-plus years later, in a garden closer to the sea, I'm still trying to learn from them and to do them justice, and I watch them these days, not only with my own eyes, but also with those of my now-departed mother, she who stood transfixed at the windows of my childhood, and all through her long and exemplary life, a child's bright wonder on her face as she observed the birds, was fascinated by birds, received across her brow the blessing of their brief, urgent, passing shadows, their tiny, undiminished ecstatic songs full of detail she could only marvel at.

* *

Pat Boran is a poet, occasional broadcaster and maker of short poetry films, which may be found at www.patboran.com. He is a member of Aosdána, Ireland's affiliation of artists and writers.

· GRATITUDE ·

Hedge School

*What's she at
   out back
that little bag
   of chirps
small beak
   hole-poking
feather-stroking
   nitpicking
stick-amassing
   her tail flashing
stitching nothing
   to nothing more
than empty air
   taking chances
with those silly dances
   playing hide and seek
on her all-alone
   and unaware
that just by being there
   in those song-sung
bone-bare
   bowed and broken branches
half her work
   is done*

Pat Boran

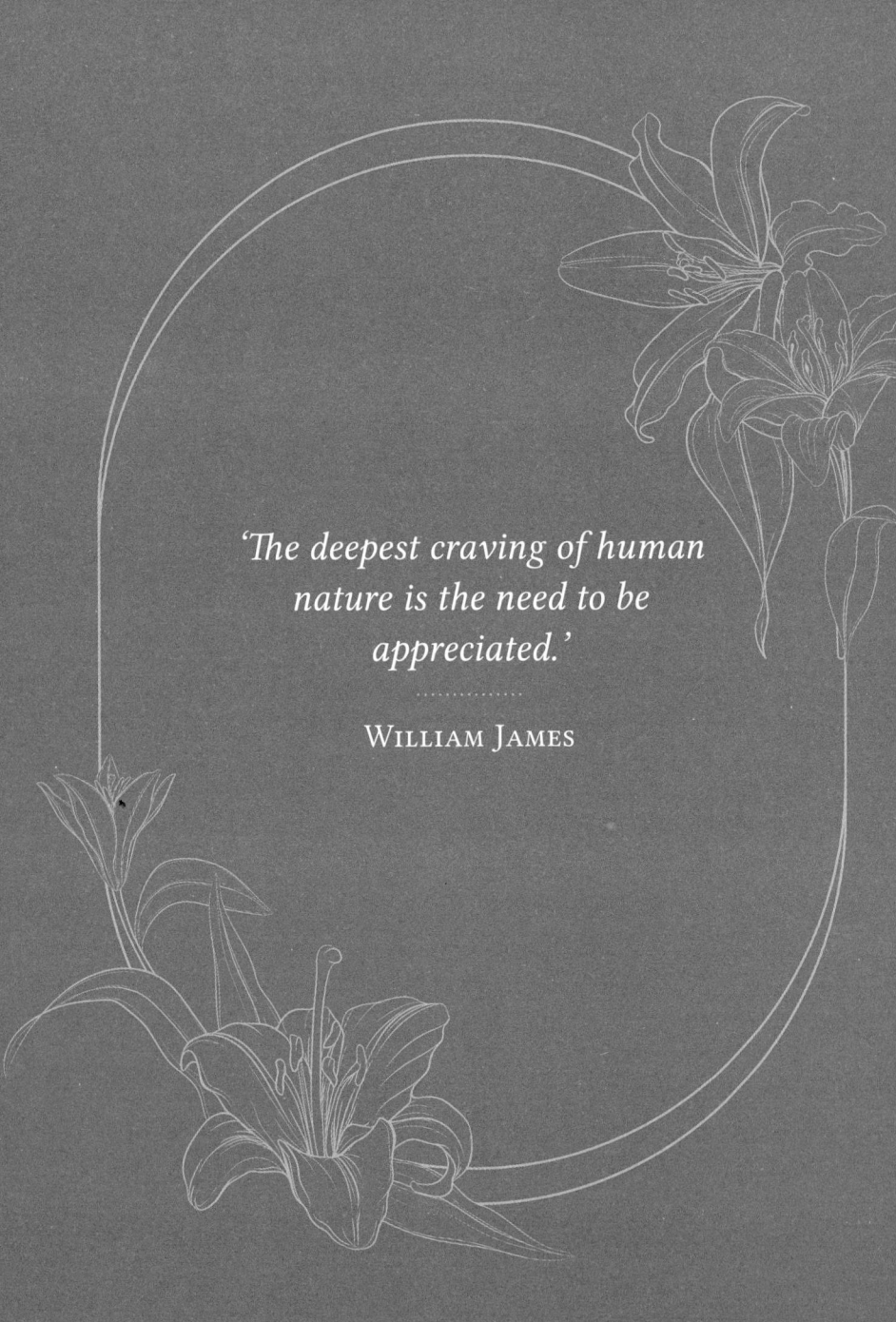

'The deepest craving of human nature is the need to be appreciated.'

WILLIAM JAMES

· GRATITUDE ·

BEING RAISED IN THE MIDDLE OF THE HOUSE

Pat Dennigan

About a week ago, Stan asked me if I would contribute a piece for her upcoming book on gratitude. 'Sure,' sez I, 'no problem. What do you want the piece to be about?'

'Gratitude. Anything whatsoever you like, whatever gratitude means to you. Just make it around 300 words' was the answer.

Easier said than done.

But the first thing that came into my head was a feeling of being fortunate, being lucky and being grateful for my parents and my upbringing. I'm 59 – born in 1965. I'm an only child and I was raised in Sligo in the West of Ireland. My granny – my mum's mum – lived with us, so there were four of us at home.

My dad had a saying from his side of the family in Longford that children should be raised in the middle of the house. Given my experience growing up, I have always taken that to mean that children should be involved in everything in the family – good and bad, normal and not so normal, happy and sad, the mundane and the wonderful. That was my experience.

My dad worked in the Post Office Engineering Branch (subsequently Telecom Éireann and now Eir). He grew vegetables, tended fruit, loved his garden and fixed any household appliance that needed fixing for ourselves and the neighbours. He was the youngest in a big family, but was the one all his family turned to for advice, help or anything else. My mum was a housewife and a homemaker. She cooked, cleaned, made jam, baked and was passionate about the GAA, and Tipperary hurling in particular. She nursed her mother, my granny, in her later years after a stroke hit when I was around twelve.

Looking back on that time, I feel immensely grateful – grateful for the home that was created for me and around me, grateful for the opportunity to grow and develop, to be educated and prepared for the rest of my life. I never realised until recently that there were such highfalutin concepts as values, but now I know that, in their own way, that is what was being passed down to me, and what I would truly love to pass to my own children.

It is something that is an integral part of me, something I carry with me all the time, and deep down something that drives me in my daily work with Focus Ireland. That sense of community and social justice is a key motivator for me to empower others. It translates into our values as an organisation of dignity, quality, social justice and empowerment.

Deep down, I suspect what we feel gratitude for is probably one of the key motivating forces we all feel.

* *

Pat Dennigan is the CEO of Focus Ireland.

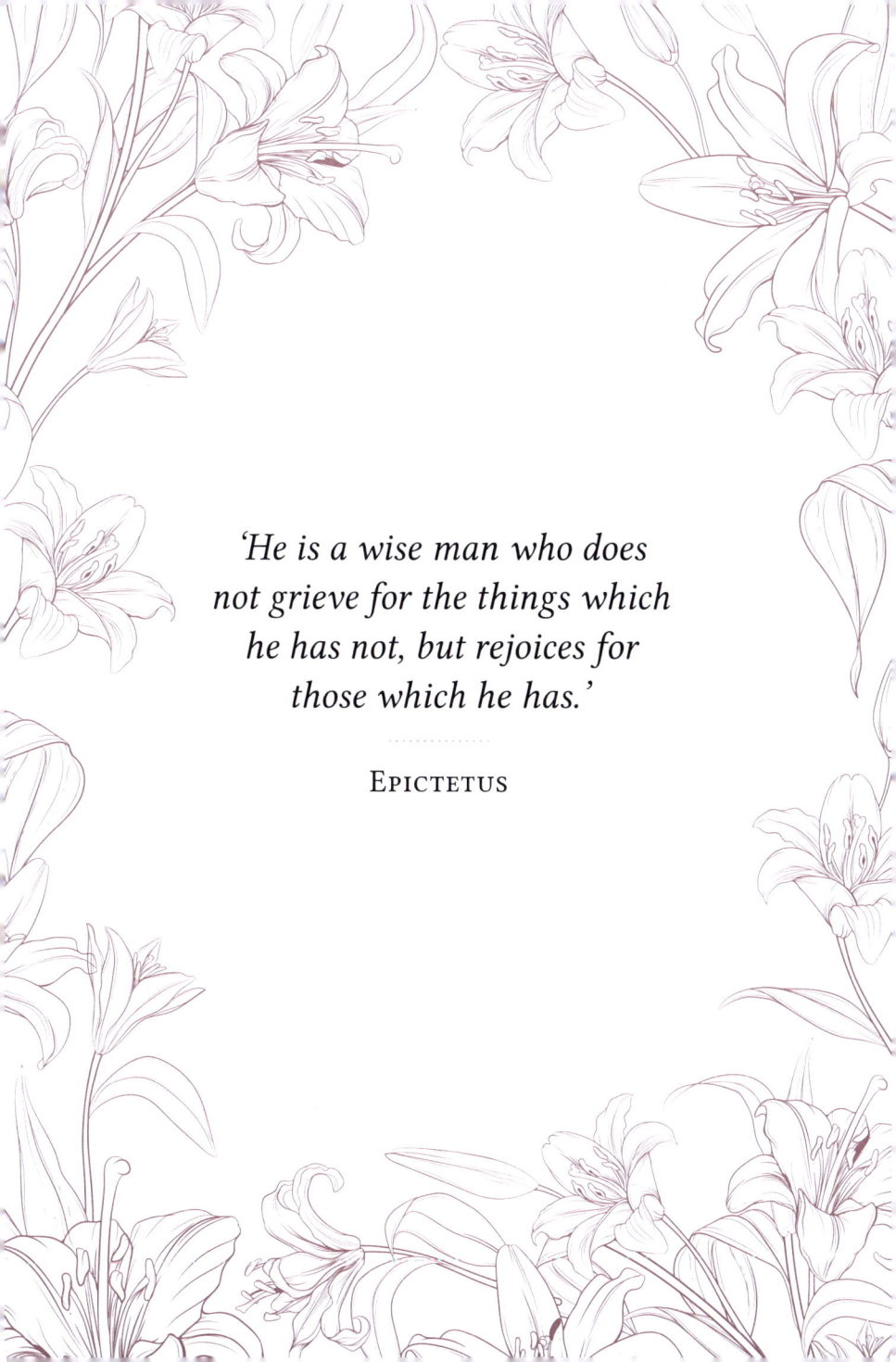

'He is a wise man who does not grieve for the things which he has not, but rejoices for those which he has.'

Epictetus

MEMORIES

Pat Spillane

The All-Ireland Final of 2022 was my last occasion appearing on *The Sunday Game*. It was the day Kerry were playing Galway, and it was probably the first time I ever cried in public, and certainly the first time I ever cried live on television.

There were several reasons for it. It was my last time appearing on *The Sunday Game*, which was emotional. My county had won the All-Ireland. People from my own area were playing; my own club, Templenoe, were playing that day. But there were two other special reasons.

My two nephews had just won their first All-Ireland medals, and, most importantly, it brought back memories of my late father, Tom.

Tom was the selector for the Kerry senior football team when Kerry played Galway in 1964.

The night before that final, walking down O'Connell Street, he got a pain in the chest, which we subsequently discovered was a slight heart attack.

He wouldn't go to the doctor or the hospital because he wanted to be in Croke Park as a selector the following day. On the Tuesday, he died from a massive heart attack.

In that one minute of television when I was crying, all the strands of my life came together – Kerry, Templenoe, but in particular family, and the death of my father; and now, two generations later, his grandsons, who he never saw and never knew, were winning All-Ireland medals.

It sums up my life and what it is all about. Gratitude to my family.

Particularly, gratitude to my mother, Maura, left widowed with four young children in her 40s with a bar and shop to run and a family to rear. A unique, warm, special person.

She parked her life for her children – never took a day off, never went shopping, never went on holidays. I have no words to express my gratitude for what my mother did for us: her love, dedication, and selflessness.

When myself and my brothers would leave the house to play in the All-Ireland, she would say to us 'remember who ye are.' That meant respect for us ourselves and respect for others.

And that's the gratitude we have – that love she had for us, and the people she made us become.

And in the rest of my life, the gratitude I feel is for family.

Gratitude to my two brothers, Tom and Mike, and my sister, Margaret. For staying together through thick and thin. For always being there in both good times and bad.

I have always been lucky in my life to be surrounded by strong, loving, supportive women.

My mother, my sister, and last but by no means least, my loving wife of 35 years, Rosarii.

I cannot with words convey my gratitude or my love for what she has done for me.

Always being there, parking her career to look after me and to rear our three beautiful children, Cara, Shóna, and Pat Junior. Now, two grandchildren later, Croía and Paddy.

Gratitude to me is about family. My mother, siblings, wife, children and grandchildren.

> *Patrick Gerard Spillane, better known as Pat Spillane, is an Irish former Gaelic football pundit and player. His league and championship career at senior level with the Kerry county team spanned seventeen years, from 1974 to 1991. Spillane is widely regarded as one of the greatest players in the history of the game. Pat has written a book, titled* In The Blood, *about his life in and out of football.*

'Gratitude is when memory is stored in the heart and not in the mind.'

Lionel Hampton

· SR STAN ·

LIVING IN THE MOMENT

Paul Cunningham

Over a decade and a half, Alzheimer's disease has taken a grip and then taken over my father's life. His sharp intellect has faded to a point that he often no longer recognises his own home, and rarely can identify the people in it.

He's been amazingly stoic as his abilities have declined – never getting angry that he had to stop playing bridge, even though he once represented Ireland in competition. He's laughed in the face of forgetfulness, rather than venting his fury and frustration.

When I visit the family home in south Dublin, he recognises that I'm someone he knows but can't quite place me. Often he concludes that I'm a former ESB colleague, another engineer who worked alongside him on rural electrification in times past. He calls me 'the tall fellow', because he can't remember my name.

His name is Connell Cunningham. He's a 90-year-old proud Donegal man who hails from Teileann in the Gaeltacht. He lives with my mother, Mary, who cares for the man before her, but sorely misses the smart, erudite and funny man that he once was. They have three children, of whom I am the youngest.

· GRATITUDE ·

When Dad and I sit by the window, and look out at the south Dublin sky, every now and again there is a glimmer of recognition. He will look and know who I am, for a fleeting moment, and then he'll smile.

And as we sip our tea and nibble our chocolate biscuits, I feel contented – and I know he does too. Then, we live in the moment, and talk about the ever-changing weather.

Paul Cunningham is political correspondent for RTÉ.

'I've had a remarkable life. I seem to be in such good places at the right time. You know, if you were to ask me to sum my life up in one word, gratitude.'

DIETRICH BONHOEFFER

· GRATITUDE ·

THREE ESSENTIAL ELEMENTS TO LIFE

Paul Johnston

Gratitude is a wonderful gift. If ever there is a day when things aren't as sunny as they might be, I take a moment to reflect on the blessings I have, and the sun returns.

I started to understand the importance of gratitude when I was a child. I was taught that there were three essential elements to prayer, and thus to life: to say thank you, and to say sorry, before asking for anything.

Each night, I like to go through the events of the day and think of all the things I have to be thankful for. Indeed, I try to do the same thing regularly, looking back over my whole life. I reflect on loving parents, a good education, the chance to have lived and worked in different countries over many years, and the good fortune to have made good friends in all of them. Above all, I'm grateful every day for having met and married the love of my life.

Being thankful also involves appreciating others, thanking them for what they do, and recognising that there are things going on in their lives, whether at work or home, that we don't always know about. I try to practice gratitude, patience, respect and understanding with people I come across, at home, at work or beyond.

I fear that the pace of life nowadays, compared to my childhood, leaves insufficient time for many important things, including gratitude. All the more important therefore to make time for it, whether through prayer or simply taking time out of the hustle and bustle of everyday life, to switch off, pause, and remember all there is to be grateful for; and, just as important, to thank others for what they do for you.

Paul Johnston is the British Ambassador to Ireland.

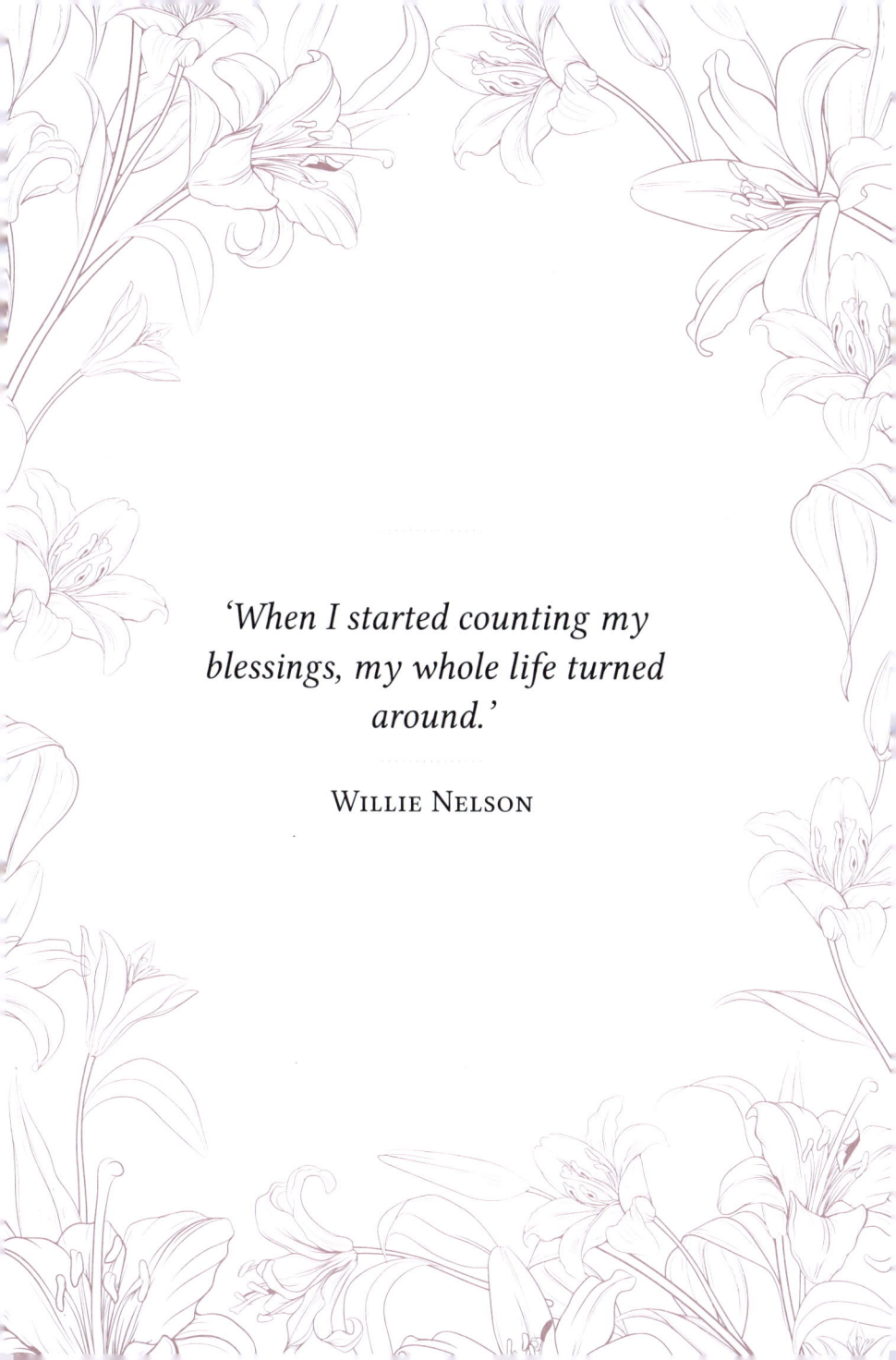

'When I started counting my blessings, my whole life turned around.'

WILLIE NELSON

STARTING SMALL

Paula Fagan

I recently met an old friend who has been working with families in distress for almost 25 years. My friend looked great and seemed very happy. We had worked together ten years before, and, as we chatted, I asked her how she had managed to remain so optimistic when seeing so much trauma all the time. 'I've seen a lot of suffering,' she replied, 'but seeing this up close has made me incredibly grateful for my own life.' She feels this every day in big and small ways, she explained, and it keeps her going.

The healing power of gratitude was clear to see in my friend, but it is not always easy to access when times are tough. Following a recent sudden bereavement, I experienced this struggle. I could list all the things I was grateful for in my head, but I couldn't feel the gratitude in my heart. So, I started small, focusing on the tiniest things that I was thankful for each day, like a hot cup of tea first thing in the morning, or hearing one of my children laughing with their friends. Reflecting on just one thing each day I felt grateful for helped me so much over those difficult months.

· GRATITUDE ·

Now, I can be grateful for the bigger things again – my family, my health, the beauty in nature, and even the time I've had with the ones I love who are no longer with us. There is always something to be grateful for each day if you take the time to notice. It is well worthwhile.

Paula Fagan is CEO of LGBT Ireland, and has been working on LGBTQI+ rights for many years. In her current role, she has overseen the expansion of the organisation and the services it provides. She was a founding board member of marriage equality, and has published several seminal research reports into the experiences of LGBTQI+ people and their family members. Paula holds an MA in Women's Studies, a HDip in Psychology, and is currently studying for an MSc in Psychotherapy.

'Gratitude unlocks the fullness of life. It turns what we have into enough, and more. It turns denial into acceptance, chaos to order, confusion to clarity. It can turn a meal into a feast, a house into a home, a stranger into a friend.'

MELODY BEATTIE

· GRATITUDE ·

MOVING COLOURS

Rachel Collier

I am lying on the stony beach in Kilcoole. There is very little sand on the surface, so the stones keep me uncomfortably awake, however tired and broken I feel.

I think back to a few months ago, when myself and my husband, Justin, walked here with our dog, Juno. The flecked stones competed for space to show off their colours, while others happily camouflaged together in masses of grey. This place, with its rough, choppy sea, rugged 'scape and sharp January rain and wind, echoes the chattering sounds of the gulls gathering along the shoreline. We lay down and looked up towards the sky. We muse over the muted blues, greens, purples, greys, which merge the sea and sky. With my hand wrapped firmly in Justin's, the cold and grey gives way to golden feelings of calm, stillness, safety, warmth and gratitude. We nurture each other. We both know that death is inevitable in the coming months, and yet we feel alive and content in these moments, flagged by such beauty.

I am grateful for colour and how it enhances every part of our lives. We walk through the colour spectrum of our walls, pictures, carpets, streets. Nature, the mother of all colour, infuses us with feelings of peace, joy and harmony with the fading from white to pink of the apple blossom, the bursting orange centre of the yellow daffodil, the wealth of forest greens. We feel the passage of time through changing colours from light to dark; from full bloom to death and renewal.

Colour brings life to places, things, feelings, time. Its beauty is intrinsic and purposeful. Like most life, it can only exist with light. Colour moves in two ways – towards light or towards darkness. The magnificent lime green leaf dons orange and brown, signifying its passage of life. It will resurface again and wave its lime light at us. Colour, like life, changes and moves towards the light again.

Kilcoole looks different today. In this longer sunlit April day, there is an abundance of green, white, yellow and blues along the seafront. The colours of this place make no sense at all to me today. My husband has died. I see little in the bright colours that can evoke a lightness of being. My feelings have moved to darker realms. My hands are blue with the cold. My aloneness goes deep and dark and seems unending. There are no golden feelings of warmth or safety, stillness or gratitude. These have left me for now. But I know life, like colour, changes and can move towards the light again. Like our clenching hands together, in time, colour will be instrumental in lifting me out of this darkness. For today though, the place and its magnificent colours surround me. 'I see you', I say and hold out my numb hand. 'I see you all. Wait.'

· ·

Rachel Collier has 40 years of experience as a social innovator. She has collaborated with Sr Stanislaus across 40 years. She helped Sr Stan when she was founding Focus Point, now Focus Ireland. Rachel also co-founded the Young Social Innovators in 2001 and was CEO for 21 years.

'The Lord is my strength and my shield; my heart trusts in him, and he helps me. My heart leaps for joy, and with my song I praise him.'

Psalm 28:7

THE FOUNDATION OF OPTIMISM

Rachel Hussey

I have always believed that gratitude is a really important emotion, and one that we should all try to practice and cultivate in our daily lives. In these troubled times, it can sometimes be challenging to stay positive and optimistic. Gratitude is a foundation of optimism, and there are always things to be grateful for, large and small. As I thought about this piece, I resolved to train myself to develop the habit of finding at least three things a day for which I am grateful and, ideally, writing them in a journal; and to remember that expressing your gratitude is a really important corollary of feeling grateful.

When I think about what I am grateful for, the overarching theme is the people in my life. Beginning with my own family, I am incredibly fortunate to have four truly fabulous children, three girls and a boy, who are all in their early 20s now. I am so grateful to be their mother, and I am so proud of the wonderful young adults they have become, each different to the others and each finding their own paths. I am grateful that I was, and continue to be, in a position to support them through their life journeys so far.

Staying with the theme of people, I am also grateful for my partner and for the wonderful friends in my life who have been with

· GRATITUDE ·

me through thick and thin, and have been an incredible support to me both at work and in my life in general. Their trust and loyalty fill me with gratitude. Whilst I am grateful for many things, at the end of the day, it is the people I am so fortunate to have in my life who generate the strongest feeling of gratitude in me.

Rachel Hussey is clients and markets partner at Arthur Cox. A former chair of the 30% Club in Ireland, she sits on the club's steering committee, and is its representative on the Review Group of Balance for Better Business. Rachel has just completed her term as president of the Irish chapter of the International Women's Forum.

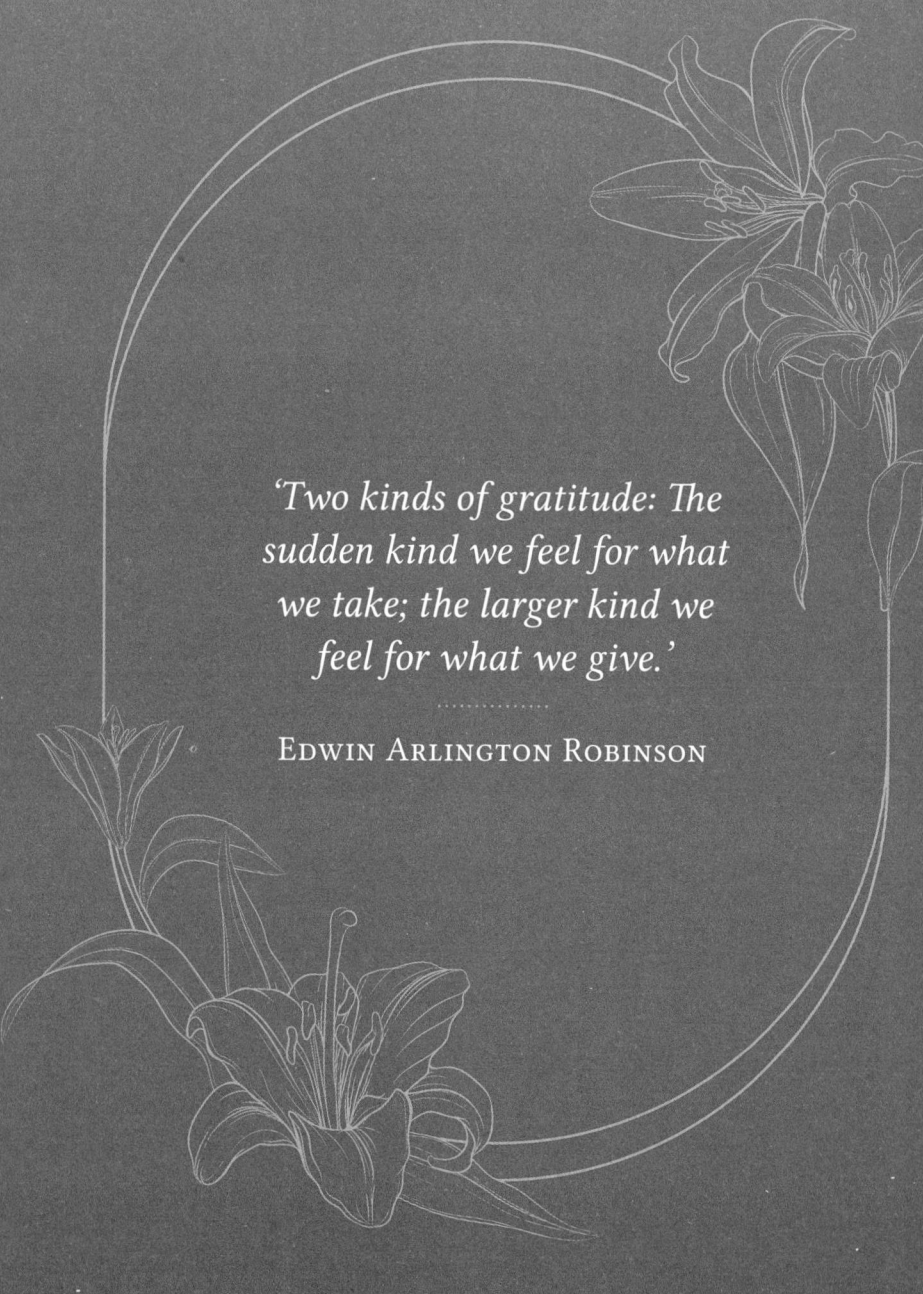

'Two kinds of gratitude: The sudden kind we feel for what we take; the larger kind we feel for what we give.'

EDWIN ARLINGTON ROBINSON

· GRATITUDE ·

MY GUIDING LIGHT

Rosanna Davison

Gratitude fills my heart as I reflect on the good fortune in my life. At the core of it all lies my family – my husband, Wesley, and our three young children, Sophia, Hugo and Oscar. They are the bedrock of love and support that sustains me through every triumph and challenge, bringing strength to my spirit. I am endlessly thankful for the bonds we share, forged in moments of joy and tested in times of challenge.

My parents, with their boundless love and guidance, have shaped me into the person I am today. Their sacrifices and encouragement have laid the foundation for my dreams to flourish, instilling in me values of compassion, resilience and integrity. I cherish the memories we've created together, from simple moments of laughter to profound conversations on their own childhoods and lives that have enriched my perspective on life.

My two younger brothers, Hubie and Michael, have always been my partners in mischief and my pillars of support. Through shared experiences and shared dreams, we have formed an unbreakable bond that fills my life with joy and meaning. Their presence is a constant source of inspiration, reminding me of the importance of connection and camaraderie.

Beyond the embrace of my immediate family and close friendships, I am deeply grateful for the gift of health. Each day, I wake up with a renewed sense of vitality, able to embrace the world with vigour and enthusiasm. The rhythm of my heartbeat, the breath in my lungs – these simple yet profound miracles remind me of the preciousness of life itself. I am thankful for the strength of my body, allowing me to pursue my career passions and navigate life's adventures.

In moments of doubt or despair, gratitude becomes my guiding light, illuminating the good that surrounds me in a world that can sometimes feel dark and difficult for people everywhere. Through the love of my family and friends, and my optimistic outlook on life, I find solace and strength to face whatever challenges lie ahead. With a heart overflowing with gratitude, I embrace each day with a sense of wonder and appreciation for the abundant blessings in my life.

· ·

Rosanna Davison is the author of the No.1 bestseller Eat Yourself Beautiful. *She was a contestant on* Dancing with the Stars (Ireland) *in 2024, and recently launched her second sustainable clothing collection with Human Collective. Rosanna currently lives in Dublin with her husband, Wesley, and their three children, Sophia, Hugo and Oscar.*

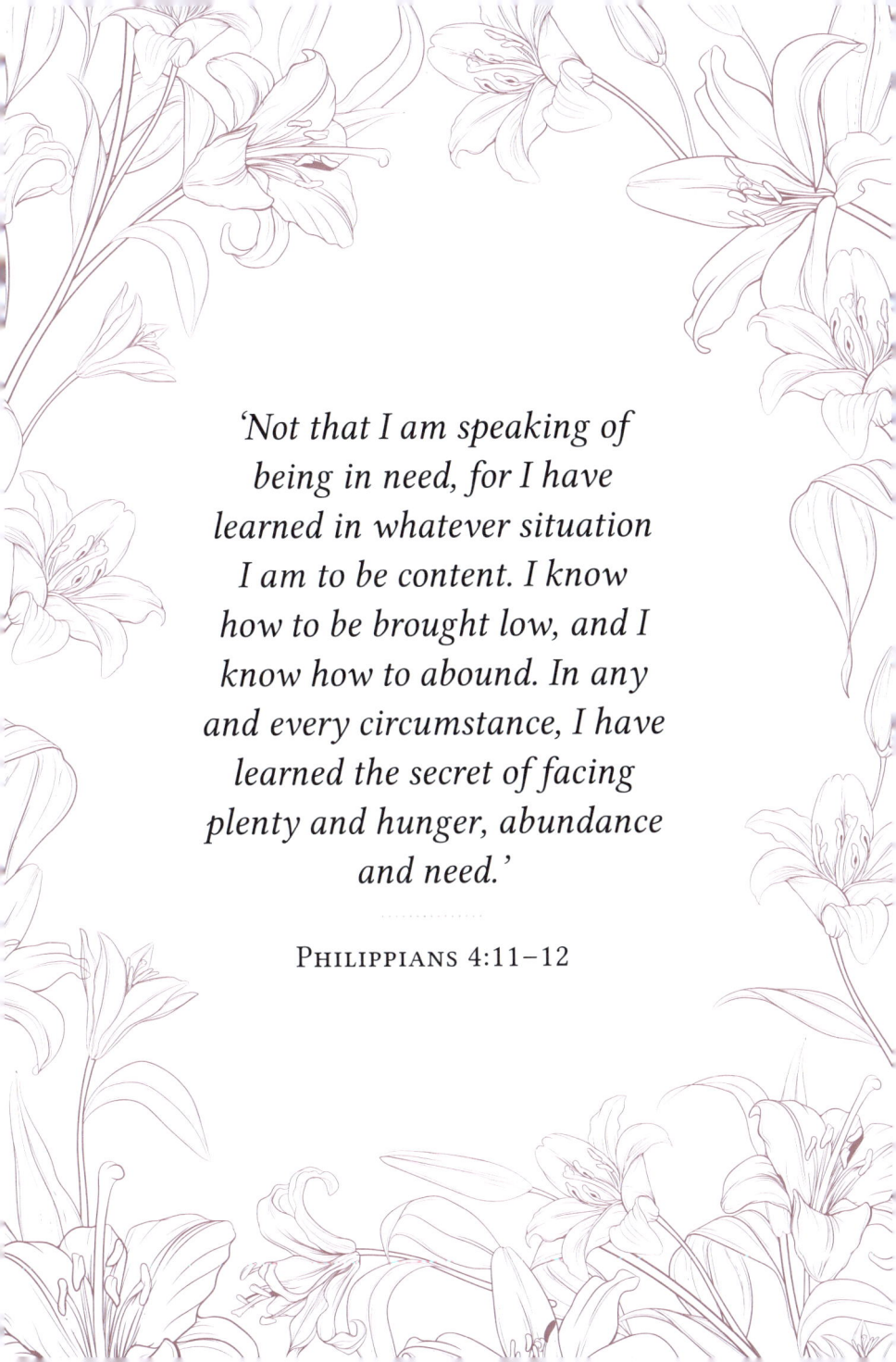

'Not that I am speaking of being in need, for I have learned in whatever situation I am to be content. I know how to be brought low, and I know how to abound. In any and every circumstance, I have learned the secret of facing plenty and hunger, abundance and need.'

Philippians 4:11–12

· SR STAN ·

THE JOY OF FRIENDSHIP

Rosita Boland

Gratitude is a big word, mostly because it is so subjective. We are also grateful for different things at different times of our lives, or so I have found. To have lived through some decades with perfect health is not something I would have given any thought to as a younger woman; but now, I am acutely aware of how grateful I am to take this for granted.

There is one enduring element of my life that has consistently provoked gratitude within me, no matter what age I have been, and that is the friendships I have.

Of all the many relationships you have in life, friendships alone are those which are entirely voluntary. They are not created through family, or marriage. Of course, you can be lucky enough to be good friends with your extended family members, but that's because there is an existing structure already in place.

Our friendships that exist outside any formal connection are based on nothing but joy. There are no shared responsibilities for finances, or children, or whose turn it is to make dinner, or bring the car to an NCT, or any of the myriad of things that bind lives in other kind of close relationships.

Our friends – or at least my friends – are the people I spend time with over long dinners, or on endless WhatsApp conversations, or sharing all manner of experiences with. Friends can make difficult situations so much better, and joyous ones even more joyous. A shared history adds up over time. They are the people who form so much of the weft and warp of our lives, and their friendships have added so much to the enjoyment and richness of my life, throughout my whole life.

Sometimes I joke that my friend quota is full, but there is always room for one more. May it always be so.

Rosita Boland is an Irish Times *reporter. She won Journalist of the Year in 2018 for her work on the Ann Lovett story.*

"Joy springs from a grateful heart. Truly, we have received much, so many graces, so any blessings, and we rejoice in this. It will do us good to think back on our lives with the grace of remembrance. Gratitude and hard work: these are two pillars of the spiritual life. Perhaps we need to ask ourselves: are we good at counting our blessings?"

Pope Francis
NYC, 24 September 2015

· GRATITUDE ·

FINDING HOME

Ross Lewis

I vividly remember my first day! White tiles, fluorescent lights, an industrial interior, steaming ovens, salamanders, solid tops full of pans, stainless steel countertops like miniature runways packed with plates. The backdrop to a frenetic home; a chorus line of cooks carefully choreographed, forming a functioning chaos held together by wilful discipline as the shouts of food orders rose above all. Excitement – pulse-raising excitement! A momentary speculation of where I fit in, but mostly a sense of place; I had found my home.

My life had taken a U-turn as I left my university years behind me in UCC to join this somewhat dysfunctional family of talented, hard-working so-called odds and misfits; these heroes and sometimes villains, their performance judged day and night with endless scrutiny.

The curtain goes up in the early morning and closes late at night, the restaurant remaining a stage in which anything and everything can happen in between. These men and women giving everything they have to offer in pursuit of perfection. Thirty-seven years on and the play still holds strong. My troop emerge through the mist of time, some vanished, some vanquished, some too old and some new; it is to them I owe my greatest gratitude, for they have made me what I am.

• •

Ross Lewis co-founded Chapter One restaurant on Parnell Square, Dublin. In February 2021, he received the inaugural Michelin Mentor Chef Award for Great Britain and Ireland.

'If you concentrate on finding whatever is good in every situation, you will discover that your life will suddenly be filled with gratitude, a feeling that nurtures the soul.'

Rabbi Harold Kushner

CREATING A DAILY ROUTINE OF GRATITUDE

Seán Gallagher

> *'Developing a daily gratitude practice costs nothing but the benefits are priceless.'*

I was recently invited by my former mentor, Jack Canfield, the well-known author of the *Chicken Soup for the Soul* book series, and the star of the movie and book *The Secret*, to join a prestigious worldwide group of coaches and speakers called the Transformational Leadership Council.

While introducing myself to the group, I began by describing myself as existing somewhere between a monk and a marketeer – one part of me loves the cut and thrust of business, and another part yearns for the solitude, simplicity and spiritual stillness of a monk.

That same ying/yang or structural tension exists in many of us, where we constantly strive to balance our career and family lives, while the incessant stream of Instagram, WhatsApp and text messages leaves little time for us to 'just be'. Similarly, our relentless pursuit of the things we feel we lack can often mean we take for granted the many blessings we already have.

Many years ago, I came to understand that the best way to cultivate gratitude was not to wait for the feeling to appear, but by developing a morning and evening gratitude practice. I start each morning with a fifteen-minute routine, before I even speak to anyone else, where I call to mind everything that I am grateful for in my life: the gift of life itself, my health, my faculties and my abilities. I close my eyes and imagine if I couldn't see, hear, walk or talk. I feel how different my life would be. When I open my eyes, I feel so blessed and grateful that I already have what many others don't have. I then feel grateful for my wife and children, my home, my friends and my work. With that in mind, every challenge or problem I will face that day fades into insignificance. At night too, I give thanks for all the opportunities and blessings I have experienced that day, so that my day starts and finishes with gratitude. For me, gratitude has become less about hoping for a feeling and more about a daily routine where, rather than reacting to life's events, I get to choose how I feel. That has made all the difference.

Seán Gallagher is a successful entrepreneur, speaker and bestselling author. A former investor on RTÉ's Dragons' Den, *he has served on the board of multiple private companies and state boards (FÁS and Intertrade Ireland). With an MBA from Ulster University, he previously qualified as a professional youth worker, and was author of the government's first life skills education programme for preventing the abuse of alcohol among young people.*

'Be thankful for what you have; you'll end up having more. If you concentrate on what you don't have, you will never, ever have enough.'

OPRAH WINFREY

· GRATITUDE ·

ACCEPTING A CONSTANT TENSION

Seán O'Sullivan

This January, I was fortunate enough to be named the BT Young Scientist and Technologist of 2024, a journey filled with essential challenges and opportunities. The exposure and connections I have been afforded from BTYSTE have been invaluable, and I'm incredibly thankful. At the exhibition, I encountered countless kind individuals, including staff (redcoats), judges and the public, who supported all students passionately through expressing a genuine interest in and desire to understand their work. Their kindness and warmth have deepened my gratitude for growing up and living in Ireland.

Inspired by Victor E. Frankel's logotherapy, I believe living well involves accepting a constant tension between where we are and where we ought to be, rather than a state of 'equilibrium'. I've been fortunate to pursue meaningful goals, guided by this philosophy, and irrespective of their perceived outcome. I am particularly grateful for the relationships I have with my family and friends, who have been a constant source of inspiration, advice and support through all of my life so far.

Everything we see was once someone's passion project, that oftentimes they pursued without understanding the full implications of their work, other than that it was their duty to realise it. I'm grateful for the opportunities and support I've received, especially from my family. I have found that reflecting upon all that has happened, and what brings my life meaning and purpose, has helped me to refine what I want out of life. I will continue practicing this gratitude in quiet moments. As a seventeen-year-old living in Ireland, I am incredibly grateful for the wonderful things that have happened in my life, and I am excited for the future that lies ahead.

● ●

Seán O'Sullivan is a seventeen-year-old living in Pallaskenry, Co. Limerick. He is currently a sixth-year student attending Coláiste Chiaráin secondary school in Croom. In January of 2024, he was announced as the winner of the 60th BT Young Scientist and Technologist Exhibition with his project entitled 'VerifyMe: A new approach to authorship attribution in the post-ChatGPT era'. He has a passion for science and technology, and believes that humanity is at the cusp of monumental change with the development of highly capable Artificial Intelligence-powered technologies.

'Bless the Lord, O my soul, and forget not all his benefits, who forgives all your iniquity, who heals all your diseases, who redeems your life from the pit, who crowns you with steadfast love and mercy, who satisfies you with good so that your youth is renewed like the eagle's.'

Psalm 103:2–5

· SR STAN ·

THE CYCLE OF THE SEASONS

Síle Wall

Now in my eighty-second year, and invited to write on gratitude in my daily life, it feels in some strange way like contributing to a eulogy at my own funeral!

The world I'm part of today is a much more complex and unpredictable place than it was when I was younger. Horrific events, acts of war and climate change are an everyday reality. Everything has sped up and not everything makes sense.

Life has become a mystery, way beyond my understanding. When I stop and reflect on being grateful, it is for me a looking back, a looking back from this moment in time; yesterday, tomorrow, or even later today, my thoughts could be different.

The loving, generous heart of my mother, and the creative free spirit of my father, both to a fault, is a moment in time that I am deeply grateful for. The gift of who I am. What a wonderful gift, the gift of life, the gift of my life.

Within the ongoing interplay between challenging and inspiring experiences, what has contributed most to my appreciation of life, without hesitation, is the difficult times. Times of struggle, loss, pain and rejection have all helped me grow into the person I am today.

Nature has also been my teacher in the context of being grateful. The metaphor of the seasons – spring, summer, autumn and winter – waiting and watching; blooming and dying; new and old; the cyclical nature of beginnings and endings. How privileged I am to be living in a green, fertile country at this time in the history of planet Earth.

Yes, for me life is a mystery from the beginning of time into an unknown future. A mystery from one moment into another moment, and my heart response is – give thanks.

Here, now, I'm alive, I've experienced, I've learned, I'm grateful. *Deo gratias.*

....

Síle Wall is a member of the congregation of Religious Sisters of Charity, founded by Mary Aikenhead in 1815. She has worked alongside Sr Stan Kennedy in the foundation and development of the sanctuary, where she continues to lead meditation practices. She co-authored The Sacred Life of Everything *and* A Quiet Space, *as well as contributing to a number of publications.*

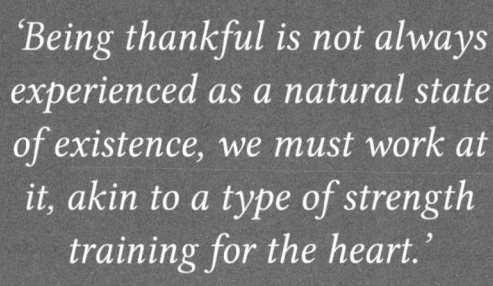

'Being thankful is not always experienced as a natural state of existence, we must work at it, akin to a type of strength training for the heart.'

LARISSA GOMEZ

· GRATITUDE ·

THE POWER OF MIDLIFE

Sonya Lennon

I am what is commonly known as a middle-aged woman. I recently started HRT, and my body is changing and ageing before my eyes.

This year, I will be thirty years with the father of my children. We never married. My mother has dementia, and my father, who is now 85, cared for her for ten years before she went into residential care during the first lockdown. He now lives alone. I'm an entrepreneur, and my business is challenging and stressful.

My twins, who are 19, are barely ever home. They are adults now, living their own lives.

What I have written above is factual. It would stand up in a court of law. Depending on your outlook and your lived experience, you might see sadness or happiness. You make your own choice to process these facts into an emotional response.

My perception of my life is that breaching a half-century is a gift, not just for still being here, but also for the opportunity to maximise the learnings, experiences and network I have amassed.

There is power in midlife: freedom and generosity, clarity and simplicity. I know what makes me happy and what builds me up. I surround myself with people who understand, love, and lift me up.

In return, I love as much as possible, share as much as possible, and support within my means.

I invest in growing my physical strength to help me live a long, healthy lifespan. I dress to amuse myself and dance whenever I can, and sometimes when I shouldn't.

My mother and father still adore each other; she is safe and happy, and he lives his life to the full. I love my work. It is a constant challenge and gives me huge rewards.

I adore watching my twins fly into their lives, and I love it for them and for me. I am free to do whatever I want. No dog will be got; this time is mine. I am so grateful for my life, health, intelligence, experiences and ability to find gratitude everywhere. It is my fuel.

· ·

Sonya Lennon (she/her) is a designer of her womenswear brand, Lennon Courtney, a multi-award-winning entrepreneur, a social entrepreneur, founding Work Equal and LIFT Ireland, and a high-profile advocate for equitable workplaces. Sonya lobbies at the European level for policy change and was recently called as an expert witness to the Joint Oireachtas Committee for Gender Equity. Sonya recently completed a Master's in Business Equity, Diversity and Inclusion in IADT.

'When we develop a right attitude of compassion and gratitude, we take a giant step towards solving our personal and international problems.'

Dalai Lama

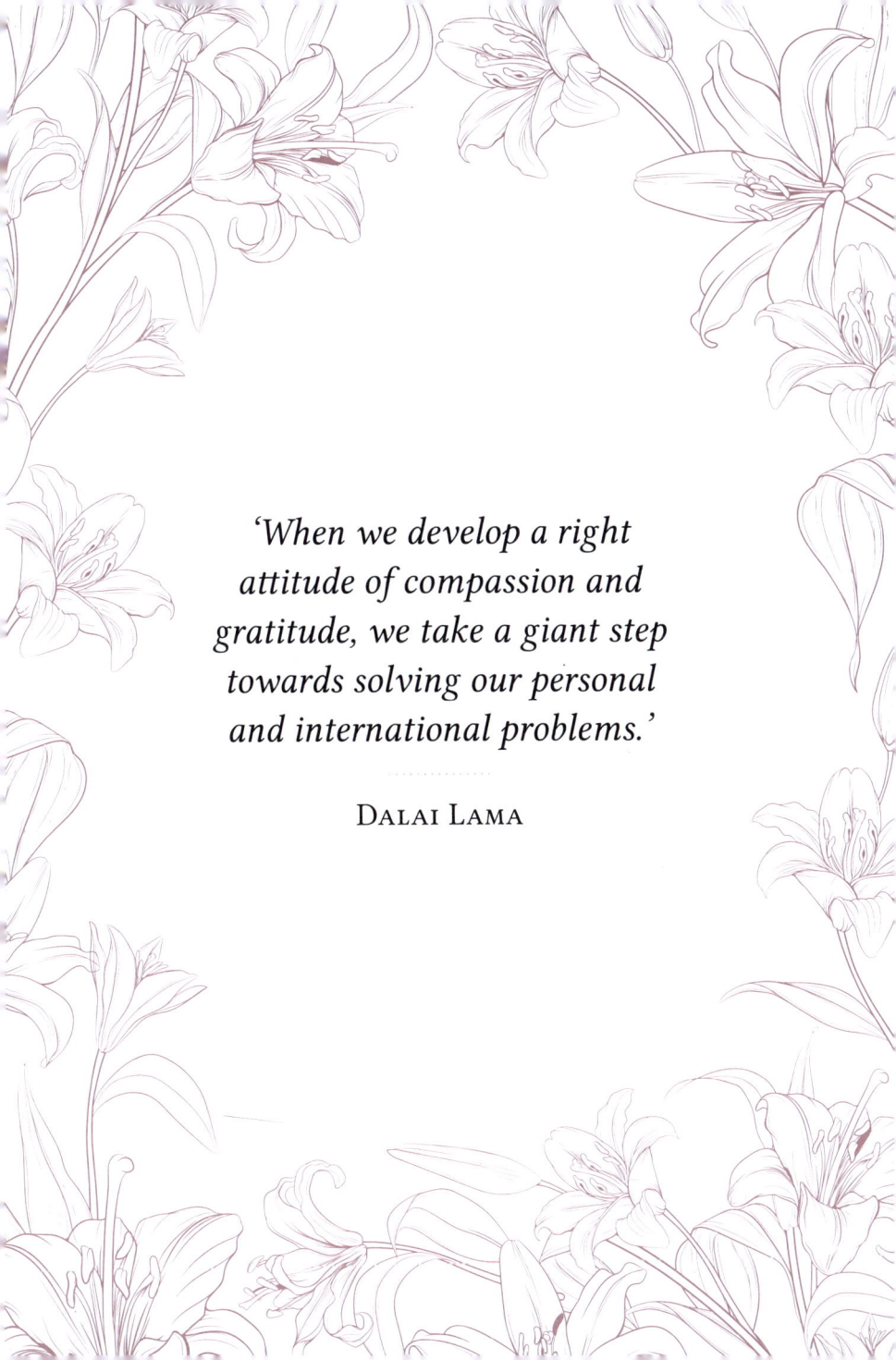

IT ALL COMES BACK TO FAMILY

Stephen Kenny

I like an empty beach in winter, walking well wrapped up, feeling the breeze on your face, that sea smell; the sound of the ocean is, I think, one of my favourite sounds in life. At Ludden Beach, you can feel rejuvenated walking close to the sea, looking across Lough Swilly towards Rathmullen, clearing the mind and allowing for a more measured perspective.

In warmer climes, running barefoot along the water's edge as the waves wash over your feet at sunset, the acceleration as you sprint to fall into the ocean on completion, a myriad of experiences leaving you fully replenished and ready for what's next.

When you are reflecting and dealing with everything life throws at you, often it comes back to family. There are families who have suffered enormous hardship or have been touched by tragedy, parents watching their children suffer through serious illness or injury, and those who have lost children and the devastation that ensues.

I am forever grateful for the health of my family, Siobhán and Niamh, Caoimhe, Fionn and Eoin. At the end of the 2014 League-winning season with Dundalk FC, we took our four, then aged between eight and fifteen, to London for a weekend with a schedule packed with art, music, football and dance to cover all of their interests. This comprised the Tate, *Billy Elliot*, Craven Cottage and *Harry Potter*. When the fifteen-year-old art student was teary-eyed and clearly moved by Monet, I laughed as I could relate to her passion. When I saw the dancer perform a solo lyrical at an event, there was a realisation that Siobhán had given hundreds of lifts to practices and, like the lads with their football and music, we are indebted to her, as I was often working away and she was the proverbial football widow.

My mother, Marie, will be 80 in December. Her and my late dad, Michael, demonstrated to us the values of hard work and the importance of family, and always showed us love whatever the circumstance. Full of gratitude.

Stephen Kenny is the former manager of the Irish international football team. He has won 16 major trophies in Ireland, has managed in 46 Champions League and Europa League games, and 40 international games.

'I looked around and thought about my life. I felt grateful. I noticed every detail. That is the key to time travel. You can only move if you are actually in the moment. You have to be where you are to get where you need to go.'

AMY POEHLER

· GRATITUDE ·

WIDENING OUR CIRCLES OF COMPASSION

Sylvia Thompson

Theoretical physicist Albert Einstein once wrote that human beings experience themselves, their thoughts and feelings as something separated from the rest of the universe, which he described as 'a kind of optimal delusion of consciousness'.

'This delusion is a kind of prison for us, restricting us to our personal desires and to affection for a few persons nearest us,' he wrote. According to Einstein, our task must be 'to free ourselves from this prison by widening our circles of compassion to embrace all living creatures and the whole of nature in its beauty.'

It is also widely held that we only protect what we love, and the recommendation from the 2021 Children and Young People's Assembly on Biodiversity Loss, that we start treating the Earth like a friend or family member, and protect it like we would a loved one suffering ill-health, is a timely reminder.

Writing in the *Irish Times* following the publication of the National Biodiversity Action Plan in February 2024, Jane Stout, Professor of Ecology at Trinity College Dublin, remarked that until we treat the earth like a friend and family member, it is not going to recover. 'If ecosystems collapse so do our livelihoods, economics and societies', she wrote.

Being grateful for this planet and its fragile abundance is an important first step towards making a conscious commitment to preventing its destruction. So perhaps my greatest desire is for humans to understand that we too are a part of the natural world, and by protecting it, we are also protecting ourselves. But, more than that, by appreciating the natural world – and being grateful for it in our everyday lives – we will bring a deeper consciousness to our efforts to reverse the decline in species and habitats, with the ultimate aim to restore a more balanced world for all to live in.

* * *

Sylvia Thompson is a journalist and author. She writes for the Irish Times *on health and environmental issues. She has an honours degree in psychology from Trinity College Dublin. Married to artist Des Fox, with three grown-up children, she is a regular sea swimmer, walker and cyclist.*

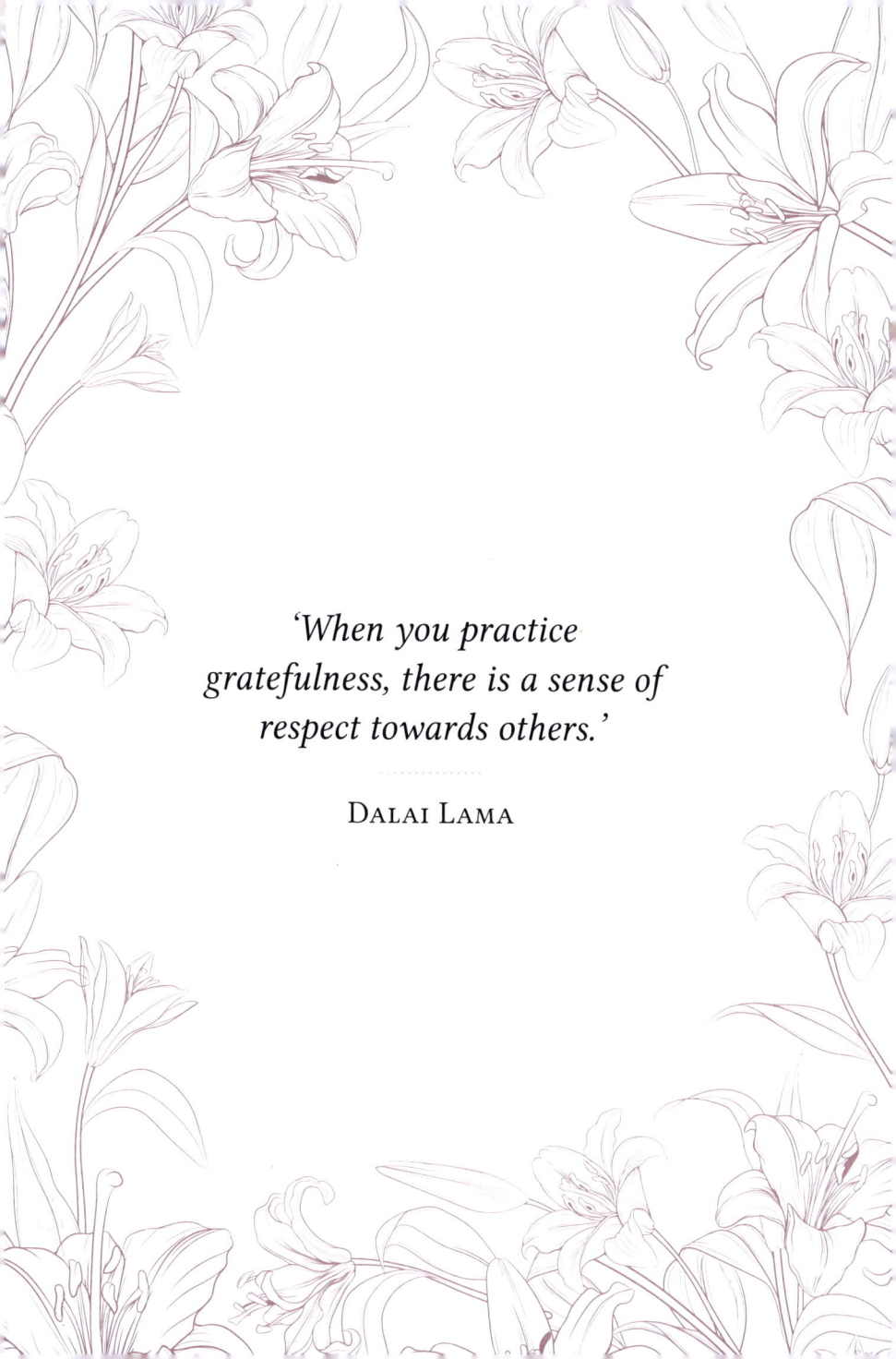

'When you practice gratefulness, there is a sense of respect towards others.'

Dalai Lama

A UNIQUE HEALING POWER

Tom O'Brien

Learning to be grateful is one of the most important life skills I have tried to acquire. It's something I work on every day. Why? Life throws its fair share of traumas, obstacles and frustrations at everyone. I'm no exception. Shortly after our daughter Katelyn was born, she was diagnosed with a very rare neurological disorder that affects one in one million children. When something like that hits you, it can be hard to be grateful for anything at first. It's easy to feel as though you've drawn the short straw in life, both for yourself and your child. That's when learning gratitude became so important for me. Gratitude possesses a unique healing power. In its simplest form, it helps you refocus on what's positive in your life. It has the ability to slowly turn adversities into sources of strength. I am so grateful for Katelyn, for the very special relationship and deep love we share. I am grateful for my wife, Máire, and how we came together after Katelyn's diagnosis, and are now stronger for it, fifteen years later. My gratitude extends to my other children, Holly and Thomas. Katelyn played a role in helping them grow into caring, patient and insightful kids. She helped us all grow.

· GRATITUDE ·

These things remind you of what's important, that life is precious and should be lived every day. Nothing should be taken for granted. It puts things into perspective. It's harder to complain about the little things (although I still do), that's why learning gratitude is something you need to work on every day. It's something I certainly try to do.

> *Tom O'Brien is managing director of an energy company. He is married to Máire, and father to Katelyn, Holly and Thomas.*

'Today I choose to live with gratitude for the love that fills my heart, the peace that rests within my spirit, and the voice of hope that says all things are possible.'

ANONYMOUS

TWO SIMPLE DISCIPLINES

Tony Keily

Sr Stan – I am so lucky
– I should feel gratitude all the time
– so why don't I?

I generally find it difficult to experience gratitude, particularly when I am distracted by unconscious fear, wanting and ego … so unless I can create some discipline around my thinking and reflect on how lucky I am, I will suffer from these negative traits. So, how do I do this?

Firstly, I have been very fortunate to have been born healthy into a lucky place, time and family. This has given me a giant step forwards in life; so to experience gratitude, I have two filters on life that I try to keep clear – the first is my relationship with myself, and the second is my relationship with the rest of the world. I try and practise two simple disciplines that allow me to keep these filters working for me.

The relationship with myself – I practise a thing called Metta Mantra meditations (look up Metta meditation – it's easy). This allows me to stay personally positive and kind to myself.

The relationship with the rest of the world – I read and re-read a book written by Anthony De Mello called *Awareness*. This book keeps me grounded, so I don't get distracted by man-made noises and concepts.

So, when I engage with these two activities, I generally feel grateful and more at peace. Do I do them every day? No, but more often than not ... thankfully!

· ·

Tony Keily is 59 years old and lives in Dublin with Catriona and their four kids (Robyn, Brandon, Georgia, Mimi ... and Django, the black Labrador). He works in a family business which is focused on 'creating better outcomes' in the health sector by means of education, training and services. He likes to think he is curious, positive and kind – and, sometimes, quick and funny!

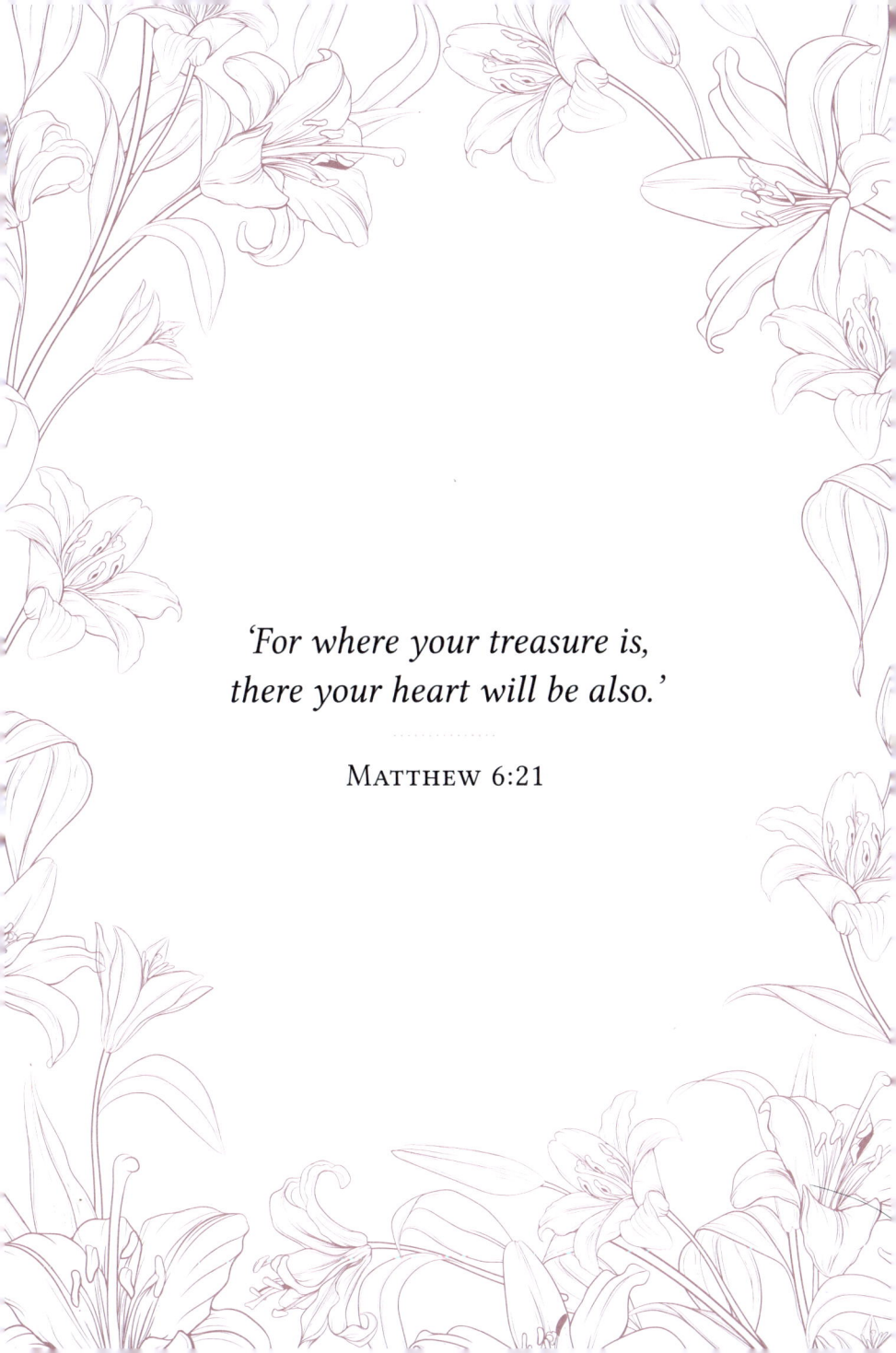

'For where your treasure is, there your heart will be also.'

Matthew 6:21

PUT YOUR OXYGEN MASK ON FIRST

Victoria Smurfit

May I tell you what I am grateful for?

1980s pop music.

Stay with me.

The music of my childhood has the ability to jump me out of any emotional dip and bring me right back to a time where joy was innate in your day. No bills, no worries, nothing to fret about, except whether or not the Angel Delight will set before my brother finds and steals it.

It is almost impossible to take any situation too seriously when Def Leppard are shouting at you to 'pour some sugar on me.' It's normal as an adult to forget to have simple joy; we're busy, juggling. However, we shouldn't. Think of it as the instruction to put your oxygen mask on first, then you can help everyone else. So find out what makes you silly? Then go for it.

· GRATITUDE ·

Gratitude means different things to all people. For me, it is about resilience and acknowledgement.

Clock that winterised tree, its twigs skinny and cold in the soft grey December light. Watch it magically flourish, slowly fattening with green as time passes. I find it's a great reminder that time comes to pass. Good things come to pass, which means so does anything troubling. Will I truly waste a season to the negative voice? The tree doesn't, its branches resiliently waiting for its next chapter, strong, bending through the storms, ready and grateful to be still there.

Every time I hear 'you didn't, you couldn't, you haven't' pinging around my head, I remember the tree, turn on the tunes, and think, I DID, I COULD, I MIGHT. Then I break a sweat and thank whoever needs thanking for rock n' pop. And silliness.

....

Victoria Smurfit is an actress for over 30 years in Ireland, the UK and the USA; a grateful mother to three; a sister, daughter and wife; and an ambassador for NCBI, Fighting Blindness, and GOSH.

'Develop an attitude
of gratitude, and give thanks
for everything that happens
to you, knowing that every
step forward is a step toward
achieving something bigger
and better than your
current situation.'

BRIAN TRACY

· GRATITUDE ·

THE GARDENING CYCLE

Will Wedge

The third-century Greek physician Galen advised practicing gratitude in our lives. When I ask myself what I am grateful for, plants, nature and gardening immediately come to mind. Of course, I am grateful for the people I love as well, but gardening has been a constant since I was eight years old, when I came to Ireland from England with my parents. Shortly after this, my parents separated; this was in the Ireland of the 1960s, and I grew up in my grandmother's dark, rambling house.

I was lost as a child in many ways, but was introduced to gardening by two old ladies, Misses Costelloe and Worthington, already in their eighties. I remember building my first rockery under their supervision. I also had three English aunts who were genius gardeners; they were meticulous, thorough and knowledgeable.

In gardening, I found myself.

Gardening is an excellent way to enter the 'now', the 'immediate'. To have your feet firmly planted in the soil is to be present in the world. It draws you out of your head and down into reality. For this, I am grateful.

Gardening leads us to an acknowledgement of the cycle of life: birth, growth, death, decay and rebirth. The beauty of plants and flowers is constantly present to us. I am grateful for the first snowdrops in spring, dahlias in summer sun, witch hazel in winter light, and seeing a spectacular oak tree all year round. I am grateful for the close contact with wildlife, from the worm to the bird in flight. To be watched intensely by a robin while digging is magic. All this before the produce from the allotment, and I am grateful for that too. Nurturing, shaping and caring for a garden brings great satisfaction and joy.

William Wedge is retired teacher after thirty-five years in education, now gardening and living happily in Dublin 7.

A GOOD DAY

Brother David Steindl-Rast

*You think this is just
    another day in your life?*

*It's not just another day;
    it's the one day that
    is given to you ...*

today

It's given to you. It's a gift.

*It's the only gift that you
    have right now, and the
    one appropriate response
    is gratefulness.*

*If you do nothing else but to
    cultivate that response to the great
    gift that this unique day is,*

· GRATITUDE ·

if you learn to respond
 as if it were the first day
 of your life,
and the very last day,

then you will have spent
 this day very well.

Begin by opening your
 eyes and be surprised that you
 have eyes you can open,

that incredible array of colors

that is constantly offered to
 us for pure enjoyment.

Look at the sky.

We so rarely look at the sky.
 We so rarely note how different
 it is from moment to
 moment with clouds coming
 and going.

SR STAN

*We just think of the weather, and
   even of the weather we don't think
   of all the many nuances of weather.*

*We just think of good weather
   and bad weather.
This day right now has
   unique weather, maybe a
   kind that will never exactly
   in that form come again.*

*That formation of clouds in the sky will
   never be the same that it is right now.*

Open your eyes. Look at that.

*Look at the faces
   of people whom you meet.*

*Each one has an incredible
   story behind their face, a story
   that you could never fully fathom,
   not only their own story,
   but the story of their ancestors.*

We all go back so far.

· GRATITUDE ·

And in this present
  moment on this day, all the
  people you meet, all that life
  from generations and from so
  many places all over the world,
  flows together and meets you
  here like a life-giving
  water, if you only open your
  heart and drink.

Open your heart
  to the incredible gifts that
  civilization gives to us.

You flip a switch
  and there is
  electric light.

You turn a faucet and
  there is warm water and cold water –
  and drinkable water.

It's a gift that millions and millions
  in the world will never experience.

So these are just a few of
an enormous number
of gifts to which you can
open your heart.

And so I wish for you that
you would open your heart
to all these blessings and let
them flow through you,
that everyone whom you will meet
on this day will be blessed by you;
just by your eyes,
by your smile, by your touch –
just by your presence.

Let the gratefulness overflow
into blessing all around you,

and then it will really be
a good day.

....
Brother David is a 90-year-old author,
scholar and Benedictine monk

· SR STAN ·

WHAT DO YOU FEEL GRATITUDE FOR IN YOUR DAILY LIFE?

Use this space to write your own thoughts on what gratitude means to you

· GRATITUDE ·

SR STAN

· GRATITUDE ·

ACKNOWLEDGEMENTS

I would like to express my heartfelt gratitude and appreciation to all those who contributed so beautifully to this book. A special thanks to my publisher, Red Stripe Press, and Michael Brennan. My thanks goes to Eileen O'Brien for editing and Alba Esteban for her beautiful design and artwork. Sincere thanks to John Cunningham, Denise Charlton, Lisa-Nicole Dunne and Roughan McNamara for all their support and assistance in identifying people to contribute. Very special thanks to Kathleen Curley-Clarke for her assistance in preparing various drafts of the book.